W9-BPL-667

Aesthetics and Nostalgia
in the Barsetshire Novels of
Angela Thirkell

by

Penelope Joan Fritzer

The Angela Thirkell Society
North America

Copyright © 2009, Penelope Joan Fritzer
First published 2009
The Angela Thirkell Society
North America
PO Box 7109
San Diego, CA 92167

All rights reserved. Except for review and/or scholarly reference, no part of this publication may be reproduced or transmitted in any form or by any means, electronic or mechanical, including photocopying, recording, or any information retrieval system without permission of the author, obtained by contacting the Angela Thirkell Society North America, PO Box 7109, San Diego, CA 92167.

Printed by   Thompson Press
              1050 Pioneer Way, Suite M
              El Cajon, CA 92020

_____

LIBRARY OF CONGRESS
CATALOGING-IN-PUBLICATION DATA
ISBN 978-0-9768345-4-0 (pbk)
I Title. Aesthetics and Nostalgia in the Barsetshire Novels of Angela Thirkell

Introduction

"Syzygy" is an astronomical term describing a perfect alignment, so by extension it is also the perfect word to describe the relationship between the three entities of Angela Thirkell readers, the Angela Thirkell Society, and the academic community. One of our members and readers, Penelope Fritzer is responsible for helping to bring together these disparate communities with common interests, and this, her latest book, is designed to reach readers of all levels of interest in the Barsetshire works of Angela Thirkell.

Strong as the interests of the readers and society founders have been, the academic community has been slower to embrace Angela Thirkell's work. Since in the long term one of the ways for her reputation to endure is through academic endorsement, it is very helpful to have the academic world involved with and exposed to the works of Angela Thirkell. Beginning with the critical book by Laura Collins, and running through other critical works by Jill Levin, Penelope Fritzer, Rachel Mather, and Jennifer Nesbitt, academics interested in Angela Thirkell have generally been both perceptive and supportive, and their books residing in college libraries around the world, along with those of Margot Strickland and Diana McFarlan, help to maintain interest in Angela Thirkell and her works. Many readers and members are proselytizers, trying their best to bring in new readers and members from various communities, so to recruit from the academic community is a natural next step.

Angela Thirkell produced 33 books in her lifetime, chronologically centered on WWII, but covering the pre-war and post-war periods. By far her most popular books are the Barsetshire series, picking up the English countryside where Trollope left off. The granddaughter of the pre-Raphaelite artist, Sir Edward Burne-Jones, she was immersed in the aesthetics of the art world during her childhood. Her father was an eminent Latin scholar, and her many relatives, such as Rudyard Kipling, are well known today. But the appeal of Angela Thirkell is of a very different sort and hard to describe. Her books are primarily descriptions of people in England doing very ordinary things. And although the characters are "county", her works touch American readers in very personal ways.

It is this personal relationship of readers to Angela Thirkell that provides a source of identification for readers today, who cover a large spectrum, from the casual Anglophile to the serious collector. This interest brings people together in the Angela Thirkell Society. In the United States, national meetings held every two years bring both avid readers and literary analysts together; the characters in the books are their mutual friends. It is at these meetings that the academic world and the enthusiasts, the serious collectors and the costumed characters (often in the same person!), all join forces in perfect syzygy.

The general membership of the Angela Thirkell Society of North America has made generous contributions over five years in support of these special book publications. Past book publications include an original Angela Thirkell play published by permission of the estate, a collection of critical essays, a previous publication by an early member of the Society (developed with the encouragement of Mrs. Thirkell's son), and a whimsical Trollope/Thirkell pastiche novel. Submissions are always welcome, as the Society selection for publication each year is based on the contribution the work makes to the interest and study of Angela Thirkell and is not, therefore, constrained by commercial considerations. The Society is extremely pleased that for this year's publication, Dr. Fritzer has offered her thoughtful analysis.

The Society also provides the valuable function of collecting original Angela Thirkell ephemera such as letters, book collections and other memorabilia, and has often been the recipients of bequests and donations of life-time collections. One of two important collections is the Mary Lois Mamer set of letters, written to her and other members of the "Thirkell Circle" by Angela Thirkell. This early group of readers eagerly waited for the Thirkell book each year, and during the war sent chocolates and stockings to Angela Thirkell. They were delighted to see mentions of these packages in the fictional work for the following year. The other important collection is the Barbara Davidson letters, contributed by Edith Jeude. Miss Davidson also corresponded with Angela Thirkell and retained both sides of the correspondence.

The Angela Thirkell Society North America is extremely pleased to have been able to place these two collections, along with other critical works and various editions of the books, with the Beinecke Rare Book & Manuscript Library at Yale University. The Beineke library is the main academic repository of Angela Thirkell materials in the United States. Gordon Haight, a Yale University librarian, arranged for Angela Thirkell to speak at Yale and to contribute papers, making the Society donation a natural extension of the Beineke's existing collection. We are hopeful of continuing to obtain original materials for the collection.

The Society prints a publication twice a year, *Divagations*, and the Society in England a yearly *Journal of the Angela Thirkell Society*. The Society in North America works extensively with the Society in England toward the common goals of sharing publications and resources.

The Society publications provide "sightings," or references to Angela Thirkell works, early reprints of some letters and articles, and other materials which make the Society publications valuable long-term references. Although these are fairly informal publications, a complete set is also included in the collection accepted by Yale University.

It is with great pleasure that we present this work by Penelope Fritzer. Her position as Academic Coordinator within the Society has enabled us to develop academic aspects to some of our activities, while remaining of interest to our more casual readers. One of the purposes of this interaction is to provide a mechanism for the long-term organization and interest in Angela Thirkell's works. I have in the past referred to works from her era of 1930-1960 as "endangered species." Without a concentrated effort at preservation, the interested reader would be left with few resources. Preservation, therefore, is a primary long term goal of the Society.

At the same time, the Society recognizes the need for fresh, contemporary thoughts and ideas about Angela Thirkell and her works. The insights provided in Dr. Fritzer's book are another contribution to the body of critical study of this author. *Aesthetics and Nostalgia in the Barsetshire Novels of Angela Thirkell* assumes a knowledge of the books and story lines. For assistance, please refer to the Angela Thirkell Society web site, www.angelathirkell.org, which provides book summaries and individual book companions, as well as other information about the author, her books, her family, and the Society.

The summaries are tucked away (www.angelathirkell.org/atbooks.htm), so as not to be obvious spoilers for those who have not read particular books.

The Society is appreciative of all who contributed to the production of this book— Terry Thompson of Thompson Press and Sue Haley and Susan Scanlon for proofreading. Andrew Binder has provided another of his charming covers, and we are extremely grateful for the efforts of this talented artist.

This work contributes seriously and significantly as a reference work for the serious study of Angela Thirkell's body of literary works. For our more casual readers, welcome to a look at the works of Angela Thirkell from a fresh, new perspective! We sincerely hope you are one of the stars in alignment as we all settle down to enjoy the pleasures of this fine book.
Barbara Houlton
Angela Thirkell Society
PO Box 7109, San Diego CA 92167

Joinats@aol.com   www.angelathirkell.org

ANDREW BINDER

Andrew Binder, the artist for the book cover, is both an educator and an artist. With a MFA from the University of Miami, he has extensive teaching and applications experience at the University level. Currently at Florida Atlantic University, he teaches multimedia classes for the Master's Degree program, and is involved with the formulation of the curriculum for the multimedia track Master's degree. He also provides technical support for the graphics artwork for the University's Web sites, as well as creating and maintaining the database and connectivity solutions for interactive web applications. His interest in Fine Arts has resulted in several limited-edition books: *Juxtaposition; The Abandoned Muse; Two Apples, Two Washing Machines, and Two Men ;and A Hearts Desire, Uncovered*. This is his second book cover for the Angela Thirkell Society, the first being *The Good Little Girls*, by Angela Thirkell.

You can view his work on the Internet:

Education site:
http://www.coe.fau.edu/abinder/

Art site:
http://www.coe.fau.edu/abinder/art/index.htm

PENELOPE JOAN FRITZER

Penelope Joan Fritzer is a professor on the Davie, Florida campus of Florida Atlantic University and the Academic Chair of the Angela Thirkell Society. She earned her B. A. in History at Connecticut College, a B. A. in Education and an M. A. in English at Florida Atlantic University, and her Ph. D. in English from the University of Miami. She is the author of numerous articles on education and of *Jane Austen and Eighteenth Century Courtesy Books*, and of *Ethnicity and Gender in the Barsetshire Novels of Anglea Thirkell*. She is the co-author of *Merry Wives and Others*: *A History of Domestic Humor Writing, Social Studies Content for Elementary and Middle School Teachers, Science Content for Elementary and Middle School Teachers, Mathematics Content for Elementary and Middle School Teachers*, and is the editor of *Character and Concept in the Barsetshire Novels of Angela Thirkell*.

TABLE OF CONTENTS

CHAPTER I: INTRODUCTION 1

CHAPTER II PRE-WAR NOVELS 11

   High Rising (1933) 11

   Wild Strawberries (1934) 16

   August Folly (1936) 18

   Summer Half (1937) 19

   Pomfret Towers (1938) 20

   The Brandons (1939) 24

   Before Lunch (1939) 27

CHAPTER III: WORLD WAR II NOVELS 30

   Cheerfulness Breaks In (1940) 30

   Northbridge Rectory (1941) 33

   Marling Hall (1942) 39

   Growing Up (1943) 43

   The Headmistress (1944) 47

   Miss Bunting (1945) 51

   Peace Breaks Out (1946) 55

CHAPTER IV: POST WAR 1946-1951 62

    Private Enterprise (1947) 62

    Love Among the Ruins (1948) 65

    The Old Bank House (1949) 68

    County Chronicle (1950) 70

    The Duke's Daughter (1951) 75

CHAPTER V: POST WAR 1952-1961 84

    Happy Return (1952) 84

    Jutland Cottage (1953) 88

    What Did It Mean? (1954) 93

    Enter Sir Robert (1955) 99

    Never Too Late (1956) 104

    A Double Affair (1957) 112

    Close Quarters (1958) 119

    Love At All Ages (1959) 126

    Three Score and Ten (1961) 134

CHAPTER VI: CONCLUSION 139

CHAPTER I: INTRODUCTION

Angela Thirkell's saga of English country life, related in her twenty-nine Barsetshire novels published between 1933 and 1961, were very popular with her contemporaries, and continue to earn new generations of readers. Despite some bitter grumbling from the occasional disenchanted critic, which grumbling has often been given disproportionate attention, most of the contemporary reviews of her novels were extremely positive, and most of the novels have held up well over the years. Laura Collins says that Thirkell describes "in arresting detail" the "decline of the life she knew and valued" (129). It is a truism by now that Thirkell's novels of manners provide remarkable documentation of social history, but there are many other elements that support their continued reputation. Jennifer Nesbitt writes in *Narrative Settlements: Geographies of British Women's Fiction Between the Wars* that of the significant women writers of the period (Angela Thirkell, Vita Sackville-West, Rebecca West, Sylvia Townsend Warner, Winifred Holtby, and Virginia Woolf), "only Thirkell remains, like Woolf, consistently in print" (17).

One of the most striking elements of Angela Thirkell's writing is her appreciation of the value of aesthetics, pertaining both to a sense of beauty and to a sense of nostalgia. In book after book, not only the Barsetshire characters, but the authorial voice as well, are concerned with aesthetics, with a sense of the beautiful and a love for the beautiful, and in many cases, the aesthetic concern is linked to the past, viewed through a lens of nostalgia. It has been noted by more than one critic that in her Barsetshire novels, Thirkell is often writing with a sensibility and a view of society that is closer in time to her parents' or grandparents' generation than it is to her own:

> Her point of view, if dated carefully, is almost that of an upper-middle class observer of a decade or so before [Thirkell's] birth and owed much to her early Burne-Jones exposure as well as her academic home. Her perspective, seen by critics as reactionary, was in fact nostalgic; she regretted not knowing a world which had never been hers but through hearsay. (Langstaff 446)

Her aesthetic appreciation seems to support that assertion, as Thirkell nostalgically finds much of her appreciation of beauty in nature and/or in the past, often both. Other strong elements of aesthetics show in her appreciation of the beauty of young children, a theme that appears in all the books, and in her many rapturous descriptions of truly beautiful architecture.

The concern for aesthetics and for the past varies in the different time periods of the various books, but it is always there. Certainly, it is less present at the start of the Barsetshire saga, in the eight pre-war novels. The seven war novels have more compelling external events, although the war atmosphere leads to appreciation of all things English. The fourteen post war novels are more distopian (the opposite of utopian), as in them Thirkell's dislike for post-war society (including its aesthetics) is uppermost, so that in these later novels the aesthetic concern is very strong in the nostalgic element for all that is lost.

But throughout her oeuvre, Thirkell is greatly concerned with aesthetics and beauty (and with the specific lack of those elements when notable), not in the strict sense of a school of philosophy, but in the sense of setting, tone, atmosphere, speech, taste, and personal appearance and grooming. The definition of "aesthetic" as "relating to the beautiful, appreciative of or responsive to the beautiful" is the one that will be implied in this study. It is a general definition that will be used in quite an elastic sense, encompassing many different areas of concern.

Although Thirkell is extraordinarily concerned with the visual aspects of aesthetics, she gives relatively little emphasis to fine art, despite her family heritage, and it is only in the later books that she pays much attention to music, despite the fact that she took both singing lessons and piano lessons and painted (Strickland 11, 16, 19). According to Margot Strickland, Thirkell spent six months in Paris and studied music in Germany (20), where "She grew to love Schubert and Wagner, Schumann and Beethoven and Brahms," and later "[S]he sang the French and German songs she had learned abroad, playing her own accompaniment at the piano" (20-21).

So just as Thirkell often divagates, the researcher reading the Barsetshire novels in their entirety inevitably finds rich areas of investigation that do not fall in strict lines, but rather infuse the whole with a deliberate period flavor, for good or for bad, that flavor often based on elements of taste and beauty, or often, as noted, the lack thereof.

Thirkell's antenna for aesthetics is so strong that she has great comedic fun with ugliness, often positing the world as a titanic struggle between beauty, represented by the natural, rural past, and ugliness, represented by the man-made, industrial present. But besides nature, the strongest element of beauty presented, and the greatest appreciation shown, is for the human endeavor of architecture. Good architecture represents everything that is good in human nature, and often the tastes of the lower and middle classes are satirized through an examination of their enthusiastic adoption of unaesthetic aspects of architecture and other material culture.

But Thirkell also has a strong feeling for tradition, and she has great fun with upper class people of education and taste being stuck living in their hideous, Victorian ancestral piles. These books were written before the resurgence in popularity of richly ornamented and solidly built Victorian architecture. Such great houses as Beliers Priory, Gatherum Castle, and Pomfret Towers, are each described many times in derogatory terms, usually by their owners in comic despair. Such situating points up a nice dichotomy between the upper-class taste for the late eighteenth and early nineteenth century beauty of such houses as the Old Bank House and Mr. Macpherson's Regency gem, and many upper class characters being stuck living in the mid- and late-nineteenth century ugliness of houses such as those cited above.

A comparable dichotomy appears between the beautiful Barchester Cathedral, described many times in loving aesthetic terms (some lesser churches also come in for similar admiration), and the hideous Southbridge School, which with every mention seems to gain more awful elements. Characters of taste recognize the difference and soldier on as necessary in their ugly houses and churches, often clinging to the old form of the Anglican service to hold on to beauty, while those of lesser taste are shown as simply oblivious.

Interestingly, taste does not always translate into kindliness. David Leslie, Geoffrey

Harvey, and Oliver Marling are all men of exquisite taste, especially (and humorously) offended by tasteless decoration and are great appreciators of "camp," but they are not especially admirable characters. By contrast, Sam Adams' taste reflects his character by improving as he does, and what sets the seal on his acceptance and makes him eligible for Lucy Marling is his very sensitive and appreciative approach to restoring the Old Bank House. By saving and supporting beauty in traditional architecture, he aligns himself with the traditions and tastes of the upper class.

Because Thirkell is so interested in architecture and especially in country house architecture, many of Richard Gill's remarks in *Happy Rural Seat: The English Country House and the Literary Imagination*, about such houses both between the wars and after World War II, are particularly apt. Gill cites George Bernard Shaw's play *Heartbreak House* as the first of a series of derogatory satires about English country life that were popular between the wars. He notes that for Aldous Huxley, Victoria Sackville-West, the early Evelyn Waugh, D. H. Lawrence, and Christopher Isherwood, "The apparent doom of the country house, which elicited from others a poignant nostalgia and even tragic sense of loss, became for them the occasion of mordant comedy. . . . [A] foolish parody of the community it once was" (135). There were, of course, exceptions, even among these writers, and one early one was *Knole and the Sackvilles*, Sackville-West's "gracious account of her famous home and its history," published in 1922 (167).

Gill points out that other writers, such as Henry James and William Butler Yeats, are consistently more admiring, and that Yeats in particular "finds in the rich man's flowering lawns, peacock and old terraces, great chambers and long galleries, images suggesting the human possibilities of which poets dream," and that some of his poems are "elegies to a vanishing order that rebuke the anarchy and rootlessness of the present" (136), a remark that seems particularly apropos of Thirkell's approach.

Similarly, as the first war receded and the second one threatened, Gill says that other writers became more elegiac about the passing of the great English country houses, so that Elizabeth Bowen, Virginia Woolf, Joyce Cary, Henry Green, and Evelyn Waugh "turned to the house with a new seriousness" (136). Gill says that "Almost in symphonic counterplay, there were statements of nostalgia, veneration, and lament" (167), but it is surprising that he never mentions Thirkell. Apparently, he is concerned only with "literary" novels, for neither does he reference P. G. Wodehouse and his comic novels, nor Agatha Christie and her mysteries, many of whose books in both cases are built around great country houses and those who inhabit them in even more of a

"Cloud Cuckoo-Land" than Thirkell's Barsetshire.

Not so tolerant of the upper class obsession with English country houses is Nick Hornby, who is converted against his will:

> I have taken the view that life is too short to spend any time worrying about the travails of the English upper classes. If you had spent the last half century listening to the strangled vows [sic] and unexamined, usually very dim assumptions that frequently emerge from the mouths of a certain kind of Englishman, you'd feel entitled to a little bit of inverted snobbery.

> I'm not sure then, quite how I was persuaded to read *In My Father's House*, Miranda Seymour's memoir about her extraordinary father and his almost demented devotion to Thrumpton Hall, the stately home he came to inherit . . . [and of which his daughter says "He gave his life to save a house"] . . . . It's a terrific story, and Miranda Seymour is too good a writer not to recognize its peculiarities and its worth. (57-58)

Country houses are, of course, central to Thirkell's work, and she admires their inhabitants almost as much as she admires their architecture (or despairs of it in a few cases such as Pomfret Towers, Gatherum Castle, and Beliers Priory, in no particular order of ugliness). Nancy Armstrong in *Desire and Domestic Fiction* points out that for some authors "the country house should be the site of the ideal household" and should offer "a model that would be realized in any and all respectable households" (69). She suggests that they support the "powerful tradition having to do with the practice of hospitality in the countryside" (71), perhaps the reason why the Bishop's and Old Lady Norton's separate instances of stinginess earn such opprobrium.

To return to Sam Adams, despite his newcomer, social outsider status, he makes clear that he will not be a marauder who tramples over traditional tastes or standards, but rather will adopt them. His forays into "good" wine surprise Mr. Marling and others with his excellent acquired taste, as do his increasingly toned down clothes. Similarly, as the Parkinsons become increasingly acceptable, their house improves (*Close Quarters*), as does their appearance (but not their speech!), and they align themselves with tradition in their aspirations. Other characters, such as Mrs. Turner, the Crofts, and the Millers, never gain much aesthetic sensibility, although they emphatically do not exhibit lower or middle class aesthetic taste, but are excused from further aesthetic achievement because of their true goodness and kindness

Despite those few neutral characters, Thirkell is interested enough in the aesthetics of beauty, and in its downside of ugliness, that material culture, the accoutrements of everyday living, from interior decoration to personal adornment, is as often presented in a negative fashion as it is in a positive one. Further, nature's aesthetic accomplishments in all forms (views, weather, and babies are three of her favorites) are repeatedly referenced, often with a view to supporting a particular element of nostalgia.

Angela Thirkell, then, was a brilliant chronicler of the times in which she lived and of the conditions of the classes of which she writes, ranging from lower to upper, with her greatest admiration for English pastoral beauty and traditional architecture. Perhaps the most humor in her references to material culture is saved for the excrescences typically admired by the lower and middle classes as representing the height of aesthetic beauty, and those despaired of by the upper classes as representing the nadir.

CHAPTER II PRE-WAR NOVELS

The novels to be examined first in relation to Thirkell's concern with aesthetics and nostalgia are the eight pre-war ones: *High Rising, Wild Strawberries, The Demon in the House, August Folly, Summer Half, Pomfret Towers, The Brandons,* and *Before Lunch.* Many of Thirkell's readers have read her Barsetshire novels multiple times, and have a vision of Barsetshire in general, formed by the descriptions and information presented in all twenty-nine novels. Therefore, it may be a distinct surprise to realize that the eight pre-war novels have in them little of the lyrical description of and longing for traditional England that one associates so strongly with Thirkell.

High Rising (1933)

As Cynthia Snowden notes, *High Rising* does not specifically mention Barsetshire (xi), although it is later revealed as the first of the Barsetshire series, dealing as it does with such prominent and recurring Barsetshire characters as Mrs. Morland, her son Tony, the Birketts and their daughters Rose and Geraldine, and with more minor characters such as the writer George Knox and his daughter Sybil, Mrs. Morland's helper Anne Todd, the publisher

Adrian Coates, and George Knox's awful secretary Una Grey.

Most of the aesthetic appreciation in this particular book relates to young Tony Morland. One notable exception is when Mrs. Morland explains to Tony, as she exhorts him to get ready for church on Christmas over his objections, "One ought to have the [Anglican] Church Service as part of one's background on account of the beauty of the language" (107), and another concerns Mrs. Morland's appreciation of the beauty of the English countryside as represented by George Knox's house at sunset, complete with her wry response to her own aesthetic reaction: "It couldn't have been better arranged, George . . Perfect setting for author, down to the robin" (126).

But, as noted, it is the descriptions of Tony Morland that most expose Thirkell's concern with aesthetics in this particular book, as she describes "little boys all [looking] exactly alike, with hair twirling round and round from a starting point on the backs of their heads, round bulging cheeks, and napes that still have some of the charm of the nursery about them" (6). This appreciation of the backs of young boys' necks and the charm of their hair turns up in various other later books as well.

It is pretty generally accepted by critics and readers alike that Tony is a stand-in for Thirkell's youngest son, Lance, just as it is accepted that Mrs. Morland is a representation of Angela Thirkell herself, so Thirkell seems to have been expressing some of her affection for and exasperation with Tony and/or her two other sons in her depiction of Mrs. Morland's responses to Tony. Lance Thirkell would have been twelve years old when *High Rising* was published in 1933, and, of course, Thirkell clearly had a strong remembrance of her maternal experience in raising the two older boys.

Those who know Thirkell well through her books know she does not fawn or gush, so, like the ironic comments that she puts into Mrs. Morland's mouth about the beauty of George Knox's setting, the aforementioned delightful description of the backs of the little boys' heads is followed by a more typical observation about "why one's offspring are under some kind of compulsion to alienate one's affections at first sight by their conceit, egoism and appalling self-satisfaction" (6). These statements set the tone for Thirkell's attitude toward children throughout the series, and are emphasized in this early book when young Tony "look[ed] so seraphic that his mother had to concentrate her mind on his disgusting [brilliantined] hair and [dirty] suit to keep herself from hugging him on the spot" (12). Additionally, "He returned from school rather more self-centered than before, talking even more, and, if possible, less interestingly. Why the other boys hadn't killed him, his doting mother couldn't conceive" (24). Dr. Ford, too, counters any tendency at sentiment, repeatedly telling Tony to "Shut up," and referring to Tony and to Dora Gould in *Demon in the House* as "Horrid little pigs, both of you" (172).

Thirkell also uses a phrase about Tony which appears in descriptions of the young in her other books: "rose-petal jelly," as in "His cheeks so cool and firm in the day, had turned to softest rose-petal jelly, and looked as if they might melt upon the pillow" (*High Rising* 41). Similarly, affection and aesthetics show in her comments about the sturdiness of little boys contrasted with the frailty of their necks (150). Much as Thirkell shows her aesthetic sensibility about boys in this book, other aesthetic concerns are largely lacking.

As an aside, an oddity worth noting in *High Rising* is Thirkell's persistent reference to Tony, his friend Robert Wesendonck, and Rose and Dora Gould as "little boys" and "little girls," when Tony and "Donk" are thirteen, Dora twelve, and Rose fourteen. These references, combined with their very young behavior and conversation, cause the reader to keep checking back to see if she has got their ages confused, but such is not the case. In rereading the novels in close order, one discovers certain verities. It is amazing, for example, just how ubiquitous Tony Morland is in the eight pre-war novels. The very young Tony is a major character in *High Rising* and in the very similar *Demon in the House*, and he appears in many of the other books, especially those dealing with Southbridge School, as a minor character.

High Rising shares with *County Chronicle* the distinction of being one of only two of the books with an actual villain (throughout the series, the Bishop, his wife, Lady Norton and Sir Ogilvy Hibberd are disliked but too flimsy to be villains). Just as Geoffrey Harvey is the scourge of Tom Grantly in the latter, Una Grey arraigns herself against the local society in the former. A very pretty, young secretary, she is disdained for almost everything except her manner of speech, which is "that faintly exaggerated [Irish] brogue which is so attractive to an English ear when politics are not involved" (*High Rising* 162).

The Demon in the House (1934)

The Demon in the House, although preceded by *Wild Strawberries*, follows much the same format, and the only new aesthetic ground is Tony's very strong reaction to a scene of natural beauty, as he looks from a new angle at the green lake, the trees, the people in the distance, and hears music borne on the air: " 'Paradise Pool,' he said softly to himself" (126-27).

Thirkell often has Mrs. Morland say of herself that she writes the same book over and over, as Thirkell has done here with *Demon in the House* seeming like the second half of *High Rising*. That sentiment was expressed by George Orwell in his 1940 essay on Charles Dickens: "What people always demand of a popular novelist is that he [sic] shall write the same book over and over again, forgetting that a man [sic] who would write the same book twice could not even write it once" (qtd. in Hornby 51).

Wild Strawberries (1934)

Wild Strawberries, published in 1934, between *High Rising* and *Demon in the House*, is very different as to both characters and description, and it is the book in which the idiosyncratic Leslie and Graham families are first the focus. Although there are slight and charming descriptions of Lady Agnes Graham's three children, those young people are not significant characters. Nor does Thirkell emphasize the beauty of the English countryside nor of the estate of Rushwater, which she will later describe so lyrically; here, she simply says, "Rushwater was a rather large, Gothic house . . . . it might have been worse than it was. Its only inner merits were a certain comfortable spaciousness and a wide corridor running the whole length of the top story" (18).

Rather, in this book Thirkell first comes into her own with the element of nostalgia, describing dead loved ones in a very evocative and nostalgic way:

Never did Emily Leslie sit in her pew without thinking of the beloved dead: her first-born buried in France [killed in World War I], and John's wife Gay, who after one year of happiness had left him wifeless and childless. . . . (12)

Her son John Leslie carries on despite his grief, but he feel great anguish about his young wife's death. By the end of the book, when John has fallen in love with Mary Preston, he can hardly believe that he is gradually forgetting Gay: "Someone whom he had loved past words was becoming a gentle shade, melting away" (173-74).

That first-born referenced by Lady Emily Leslie is mentioned throughout *Wild Strawberries*, always with a wistful nostalgia, culminating in the morning of the birthday party for Martin Leslie, son of that long-dead Giles Leslie. Thirkell writes:

"It brings it back," said Mr. Leslie. "Wish it could bring other things back. Martin gets more like him every day, Emily.

When I heard Martin's voice on the stairs this morning, I could have believed--Oh, well, must get down to breakfast," said Mr. Leslie, blowing his nose. (167)

These heartrending and nostalgic descriptions of feelings so familiar to those who have lost loved ones, mark a very different approach to death than do the casual references to Mrs. Morland's or George Knox's little-missed spouses in the earlier books, or the humorous descriptions of Mrs. Brandon's feelings about her deceased husband in later ones.

August Folly (1936)

August Folly, a more light-hearted book, is heavier on personal description than on nature or architecture. A throwback to *High Rising* has Margaret Tebben find "so endearing . . . the way [Lawrence Palmer's] hair grew at the back of his neck" (359). Throughout, there is much admiration of Mrs. Dean's appearance and dress, but not much nostalgia. Interestingly, the most aesthetically evocative passage in the book involves one of the most minor characters, in the description of natural beauty leading up to Helen Dean's engagement:

The library was in darkness, except for moonlight pouring through the high windows. The door into the garden was open and she stepped out into the strange brilliance of the moon. The grass was soft to tread, the night-scented flowers heavy on the air. She walked across the lawn to where the lily- pond lay, molten silver with a marble edge .... Softly she trod the stone walk towards [Charles Fanshawe], the faint sound of her footsteps drowned by the splash of the little fountain that flung diamonds toward the moon. . . . (389-393)

Summer Half (1937)

Summer Half, perhaps because it is largely set in a school, and so looks forward rather than back, contains virtually no nostalgia and no passages extolling aesthetics, even those of the "admiring boys" variety, despite the fact that the book is full of boys. These boys, including Tony Morland, are sixteenish and so presumably have lost much of their babyish physical appeal.

Rather, the greatest theme of beauty throughout *Summer Half* is the ongoing admiration of Rose Birkett, and that admiration is clearly only for her physical charms, as character after character disparages her intelligence, criticizes her manners, and emphasizes her shallowness. Interestingly for one so beautiful, neither can she dance well

(88), in contrast to Kate Keith, whose physical gracefulness is representative of her graceful manners and kind heart. Except for Philip Winter, neither the boys, the masters, nor the other adults care much for Rose. Colin Keith, acknowledging both her beauty and her boringness, even refers to her as "that waxwork" (88). Rose "was certainly a ravishing creature, with every attribute of fair wavy hair, dark eyebrows, huge blue eyes, elegant figure, and unexceptionable legs" (30), none of which make up for her silliness, her slang, her pouts, or her lack of talent on the ocarina. Thirkell will, in fact, relent in later years, and have Rose mature into a kind and generous woman in *Jutland Cottage*, but in these early books, she is almost universally disdained despite her striking beauty.

Pomfret Towers (1938)

Pomfret Towers is much heavier on both aesthetics and nostalgia than are the other early books. In the opening pages of the book, Thirkell shows the lyrical descriptive powers that make elements of her writing so memorable, as she describes her picturesque English town of Nutfield, emphasizing that much of its beauty is both antique and under threat from the modem world, protected only by Lord Pomfret's fierce eccentricity (11-12).

Although many of the aesthetic references throughout the novel relate to the hideousness of the Towers, in several of the most poignant passages, Thirkell lovingly describes the beauty of the architect Mr. Barton's house Mellings, the dower house he rents from Lord Pomfret, and she shows how Mr. Barton's love of beauty helps him stave off loneliness:

> Of all this Mr. Barton was a passionate lover and faithful guardian, finding it of infinite comfort when his wife seemed farther away than usual . . . . When at rare intervals, he allowed himself to feel that something was wanting [in his marriage], he took refuge in the beauty of his house. . . . [He]might be found at odd times in the drawing room, filling his eyes with the charm of the exquisitely proportioned white panels, or on the stairs, affectionately fingering the carved balustrade, absorbing from their quiet beauty something that restored him to his usual outward calm. (13-15)

When his beloved daughter Alice is going to travel to Italy with her mother, he has a similar reaction (213), as he does near the end of the book: "The lease of Mellings would see him through his lifetime, and while Mellings was there, the world was not entirely empty" (315-16).

Through such passages as the above, Thirkell shows her strong sense of the power of beauty. Similarly, in the same book, in a passage reminiscent of the Leslies' sorrow for their son killed in World War I, Thirkell shows how loss of a loved one, and continued nostalgia for that loved one, has affected Lady Pomfret's life. She visits with Mrs. Barton: "Seeing Alice had reminded [Lady Pomfret] of the days before sorrow had broken her health and driven her into herself . . . . No tears were shed for what had happened so long ago, but both women were moved by their evocation of the past. . . "(254)

Lady Pomfret alludes several times throughout the book to the fact that because of her sorrow, she spends too much time abroad and has not been a help to her husband in his position in the county, but when she welcomes Sally Wicklow as Gillie Foster's bride, Lady Pomfret tries to make that absence up to her husband (280).

Alice Barton paints charmingly, apparently in a rather gentle, traditional representational style, so although her work is presented positively, it is slight compared to that of Julian Rivers. Jill Levin points out that "[W]hen [Thirkell] wanted to portray a serious artist [of any medium] in the Barsetshire novels, the character was always made at least nominally male . . . . The women in her books who write, write popular fluff" (26). Even Mrs.

Barton here in *Pomfret Towers*, chronicler of papal history, is a historical novelist. Despite the harsh remarks about Julian Rivers, he will make a serious art career in the public arena, while Alice Barton, whose drawings and paintings are much more charming, will be a dilettante.

Thirkell comments amusingly on the contemporary art scene, using Julian Rivers as her point man, and mocking his efforts and those of his contemporaries, the Set of Five, throughout. Although she was close to her grandfather Edward Burne-Jones and proud of his artistic accomplishments, the reputation of the pre-Raphaelites had faded (and not yet been rehabilitated) while Thirkell was writing, so her remarks about art tend rather toward denigrating modern art than praising art of the past.

Oddly enough, fine art comes into Thirkell's books relatively seldom. She is much more interested in architecture and natural beauty, and even in [the hideousness of] many areas of popular culture, than she is in fine art, despite both her grandfather's artistic influence and having sat herself for a charcoal portrait by John Singer Sargent, a drawing by Thea Proctor, a painting by John Collier (Collins 92) and a painting by Neville Lytton (Strickland 166). Julian Rivers is a relatively minor thread throughout the books, but the other art references are even more minor.

Julian is referenced in several later books, with a rising reputation despite Barsetshire's opinion of him. During World War II, he works for the government as an official war artist (*Peace Breaks Out* 16), and later it is noted that he goes by the moniker of "Common Wealth." By *Happy Return*, he is a Professor of Culture at Lazarus College (162-63). Later, he has a gallery and is part of the Set of Five (*Close Quarters* 179). Julian's successes, while still earning the ire of Thirkell's characters, are symbolic of the rise of modern art, despite the misgivings of the representationalists.

The Brandons (1939)

The Brandons is much more frivolous in tone, despite the fact that much of the plot is built around the very secluded Miss Brandon's love of and nostalgia for her long-dead brother. Additionally, much of the aesthetic concern is negative, in the descriptions of Brandon Abbey and of its mistress Miss Amelia Brandon. In her rudeness and eccentricity, Miss Brandon is presented as something of a cartoon character, and Mrs. Brandon is the only one who really seems to understand her sister-in law's pain.

But the book still is very light, probably because of the presence of the charm-laden Lavinia Brandon and her delightfully smart-aleck son Francis, who will be presented in a more negative light in *County Chronicle*. Francis' cheerful, joking relationship with his mother, particularly in this book and later in *Private Enterprise*, is a welcome change from the rocky, if loving, relationships of many mothers and sons in Thirkell's fictional world.

An amusing contrast to Miss Brandon's nostalgia for her brother, emphasized throughout the book, is Mrs. Brandon's attitude toward her dead, dull spouse, who died early and left her well off: "As it was a cold spring, Mrs. Brandon was able to go into black, and the ensuing summer being a particularly hot one gave her an excuse for mourning in white, though she always wore a heavy necklace of old jet to show goodwill" (7-8). As if to further reinforce Mrs. Brandon's lack of nostalgia for her husband, Thirkell notes with humor and class consciousness that Mrs. Brandon could never be thankful enough that her husband had died at Cannes and been decently buried in the English cemetery, so she didn't have to bother with appropriate flowers herself (20-21).

The Brandons is one of the books in which the aesthetics of past taste, often glorified from the seventeenth and eighteenth centuries, are considered hideous from the latter nineteenth century. Although Pomfret Towers, Gatherum Castle, and Beliers Priory, all of them built in the late Victorian age, are referred to as hideous by Thirkell in various books, it is Brandon Abbey especially that is presented in a totally negative light with virtually no redeeming characteristics: the outside of the house is ugly, the inside is damp, dark, and uncomfortable, and the decoration is execrable, culminating in "a Knight Templar, with the clock face under his horse's stomach" (31-33). Nor should the reader forget the "two life-size and highly varnished black wooden statues of gorillas, wearing hats and holding out trays for visiting cards" (39).

The many descriptions of Brandon Abbey are the first instances of the very clever and detailed recounting of aesthetic horrors that will appear in later books (much like the very detailed descriptions of Mrs. Tebben's nasty food in *August Folly* and later books). Interestingly, in *The Brandons*, unlike in many of the books that follow, the aesthetic horrors are not really elements of class, but they are indictments of High Victorian taste. The descriptions of the mistress of the Abbey are almost as harsh: Miss Brandon, like Miss Pemberton later, resembles "one of the Roman Emperors" in a cheap wig or a bonnet (41).

The only other notable aesthetics in the novel relate to the various men's responses to Mrs. Brandon's prettiness, and to the charm of the outdoor summer evenings under the

Spanish chestnut tree. The following passage captures each, mocking aesthetic appreciation and flights of fancy by the love-struck Hilary Grant:

> [S]ilver candlesticks with shaded candles. . . . burnt steadily under the great Spanish chestnut. . . . Mr. Grant's soul took flight [at the beauty surrounding him]. . . Mr. Grant's soul returned suddenly to his body, but as no one had noticed its absence . . . its return passed unobserved. (67-68)

Before Lunch (1939)

The last of the pre-war novels, *Before Lunch*, contains the by-now familiar themes of loss and nostalgia, as Lord Pomfret, missing Gillie and Sally Foster's baby, remembers his own son: "[H]e thought of the six months' old baby who was later to bear the title of his only son, killed so long ago" (85). Another theme is the beauty of the countryside, as exemplified by the efforts throughout to thwart Sir Ogilvy Hibberd from buying and building on Pooker's Piece, thereby ruining the aesthetics of the area. In keeping with such appreciation of the countryside is the very flattering description of the outside of Staple Park, Lord Bond's home, and the very funny description of the inside with its gloom, its many second rate paintings, and its ghastly, over-decorated furniture (60). Lord Bond, hurrying him through the rest of the house, takes Denis Stoner to see a hideous piano in a quite beautiful room: "Denis almost gasped with pleasure at its quiet mellow beauty. . . . [Behind him] stood the largest, most hideous, most elephant-legged piano that Edwardian money could buy. (64) Again, as in *The Brandons*, the execrable taste is not a function of class, as it so often is in Thirkell's books, but of its time period, as the beautiful, probably Adam room is defiled with the Edwardian piano and decorations.

Another element of aesthetics in *Before Lunch* is Thirkell's attention to music. Lord Bond, despite his social rank, has solidly middle class taste in music, being a devotee of Gilbert and Sullivan and of Chopin, while Denis is much more avant-garde, even while admitting their charm, and he exerts himself to please Lord Bond out of kindness (42-43). Denis' kind act is its own reward when Lord Bond funds a ballet using Denis' music, giving him his start in the musical world. Denis' attention to his music is entwined with his love affair with Mrs. Middleton, but as the music grows in importance, and as Mrs. Middleton remains committed to her marriage, they take a very poignant and painful leave of each other (198-99). Thirkell also has some fun in this book with tracking down a supposedly ancient country song of great historical and musical value. When Ed Pollett is bribed by Denis

Stonor with the promise of a mouth organ if he will sing the song, it turns out to be a music-hall ditty from the 1890s.

CHAPTER III: WORLD WAR II NOVELS

Of the seven war novels, *Cheerfulness Breaks In*, *Northbridge Rectory*, *Marling Hall*, *Growing Up*, *The Headmistress*, *Miss Bunting*, and *Peace Breaks Out*, each deals with aesthetics and nostalgia in a stronger way than do most of the pre-war novels. Jennifer Nesbitt says that "Angela Thirkell consolidated her literary reputation during the Second World War, producing wistful, stalwart portraits of blacked-out villages and unity-under-petrol rationing . . . ." (18).

Cheerfulness Breaks In (1940)

In *Cheerfulness Breaks In*, the harsh contrasts between the peacefulness of the English countryside, which is not yet being bombed, and the war, which has already begun in Europe, are pointed up. Thirkell might well be a Romantic poet, as she lovingly describes the landscape in a way that is particularly archetypal:

> Nothing could have been more lovely and more peaceful . . . water meadows on one side and the downs on the other. [There was] the melancholy yet pleasing dissonance of sheep bells. . . . The short lime avenue that led to Northbridge Manor was beginning to turn yellow, and Michaelmas daisies shone in every

amethystine colour below it. It seemed quite useless to speak of this peaceful beauty, which needs must make one think of other autumn fields where the earth was red, the trees broken, the harvest ravaged. . . . (96)

Similarly, as Noel Merton bids Lydia farewell to go work at his secret base, they sit outside:

The trees were dripping their golden autumn coats onto the grass and everything breathed an undisturbed peace .... They walked down the lawn and through the little gate into the meadows. . . . The winding course of the river was marked by a fringe of alders, willows, and mountain ashes, now almost leafless, while above it rose the line of the downs with the beech clump showing its tracery against the sky. (217,219)

These kinds of descriptions are the ones that stand out in Thirkell's writing and color readers' memories of the books and mental pictures of England, and these descriptions give the various plots a strong sense of English life that carries from book to book, infusing Thirkell's entire oeuvre. *Cheerfulness Breaks In* is a powerful book in several ways: this is the only book in which the fate of a major character is left hanging, as Noel Merton is in a life or death situation at Dunkirk, a situation that is not resolved until *Northbridge Rectory* (135). Also, in addition to the lyrical descriptions of the countryside that are characteristic of her work, Thirkell gives a moving statement, in the mind of Mrs. Crawley, of the past and the future depending upon the outcome of the war, and her thoughts are some of the earliest that show both nostalgia for the past and extreme apprehension about the events that are overtaking England and about the "Brave New World" that may result from those events:

> [A]ll her broadmindedness could not make her think it would be so happy for the people of her own age who had seen the golden Edwardian prime. . . . [T]he young might inherit a world whose most enchanting pleasures they had not known and would not miss. . . . (300-301 *Cheerfulness Breaks In*)

Perhaps in keeping with the general air of unsettledness, due to the outbreak of the war, *Cheerfulness Breaks In* is also the book in which Thirkell begins her habit of having multiple characters several times nostalgically remember the events detailed in past books. Clearly, the stressful nature of the times is influencing her characters to look back rather than to look forward, as in the pre-war books. Here, the remembering begins early (14) as Lieutenant John Fairweather recalls his days at Southbridge School in *Summer Half*, goes on to Noel Merton midway through the book recalling the picnic on Parsley Island, also from *Summer Half* (279), and concludes with the Archdeacon's nameless daughter recalling Guy Barton's engagement to Phoebe Rivers in *Pomfret Towers* (313) and Lydia and Colin Keith again referencing the same picnic from *Summer Half* (321). One would expect the author of such a complex series occasionally to remind readers of past events, but the characters speaking so often and so longingly of the idyllic past imparts a real sense of nostalgia.

Northbridge Rectory (1941)

The second war novel, *Northbridge Rectory*, waxes less poetic and more pragmatic than does *Cheerfulness Breaks In*. Like that book, *Northbridge Rectory* continues the characters' constant referencing of the past, in response to the perplexities of the present. But *Northbridge Rectory* is also relentlessly local, set as it is in the small village of Northbridge and focused not on the external war, as in the last poignant pages of *Cheerfulness Breaks In*, but on the quirks and deliberately petty concerns of the cast of village characters, to the extent that one might be forgiven for wondering how the British ever won the war.

Northbridge Rectory opens with the by now familiar device of Thirkell setting the stage with a lyrical description of the beauties and eccentricities of the town. It is clear from her descriptions in the various books that she is knowledgeable about both history and architecture, and in Northbridge, she gives her readers a High Street full of old houses of "honey-colored stone . . .weathered to soft greys and browns," a Town Hall on stone legs, "great sash windows," "picturesque and insanitary cottages," and always the "lovely" (7-8) and "noble" (15) curve of the High Street, which is the model for "one or two circular staircases" in houses with "fine plaster ceilings" (8). However, being Thirkell, with irony and rue she also notes that the town is only beautiful if one ignores the "three modest monstrosities" of the row of council houses, the gasometer, and the Victorian church (7-8). Additionally, there are delightful, evocative descriptions of the belfry, the battlements, and myriad other aspects of the church tower (54).

Once Thirkell has set the general stage, the reader learns more about individual houses, as well as about the aesthetics of the owners themselves. Most of the personal descriptions tend toward the negative, as Thirkell apparently feels that the intelligence, spirit, patience, taste, and manners of her best-liked characters often need little embellishing, but she establishes some of her other characters' less admirable qualities through incisive physical description.

Despite the fact that she lives in a "charming little stone cottage," the first truly personal description is that of Miss Pemberton, whose ascetic approach is reflected in her dress of "homespun sackcloth, stout boots, and a battered felt hat" (10) and her resemblance to "an elderly man with a powerful and slightly unpleasant face . . . [and] short grey hair" (19). Mr. Villars marvels that her boarder, Mr. Downing, a man of taste and an old friend of his, can tolerate "such complete absence of charm . . . [and] revolting exterior" (13). Her physical description accurately presages the later information of that lady academic living a pinched and narrow life of scholarly devotion and of jealous domination over her lodger and sometime co-author (10). Mr. Downing is himself likened to a tame cat (his nickname between Mrs. Turner's nieces is "Pussy"), and more than once described as a "sleek grey-headed bird" (249).

While Miss Pemberton is both scholarly and dedicated, one of the most acute witticisms in the book comes from the exchange between Mr. Holden, the former employee of publisher Adrian Coates, and Mrs. Villars, when she explains that "Of course Miss Pemberton doesn't write for *money*," and he flatly replies "It wouldn't be any good if she did . . . she couldn't" (11). This little exchange is especially telling coming from Thirkell, the popular author whose books were in great demand during the war. Mr. Holden, however, will be the means by which Miss Pemberton becomes a (modestly) popular author when he recruits her to write a cookbook (187). Thirkell's very accurate aesthetic sense is again on display when she describes Miss Pemberton's rustic table setting, a perfect venue for the surprisingly delicious three-course meal she serves of similarly rustic food, showing the reader a whole new side of Miss Pemberton, whose living conditions are so uncomfortable that one is surprised to read of her domesticity in the kitchen.

The Hollies, "a pleasant stone Georgian house standing back a little from the street" (15), seems far too good for its occupants, Mrs. Turner and her two nieces. All three are kindly, hardworking, and attractive women who have neither taste, intellect, nor aesthetic sense, devoted as they are to popular music, popular periodicals, and popular drinks (cocktails). By contrast, Mrs. Villars, a lovely woman of taste and the heroine of the book, as far as it has one, lives in the rectory, "an ugly but commodious house" (9).

Another very idiosyncratic personal description is that of Mrs. Spender, whose way of speech, including nonstop talking, referring to herself in the third person, commenting in asides on her own motivations, and expressing herself in such coy phrases as "a tinty winty sherry" (71) leaves the other characters subtly marveling at how her husband stands her. Her physical description, as seen through the eyes of Mr. Villars, emphasizes her "ready-made" suit and her relentlessly matching accessories, in addition to her "terrifying vitality . . . hard, rather large mouth . . .[and] very ugly hands" (72). The reader feels rather sorry for Mrs. Spender, grateful as she is to be invited, and cheerful and helpful as she tries to be, while the other characters metaphysically roll their eyes at her gauche behavior.

The fastidious Mrs. Villars is especially put off when she is forced by Mrs. Spender to see her messy bedroom and unappetizing arrangements for carrying tea, sugar, and butter with somewhat overbearing patriotic enthusiasm. Finally, Mrs. Spender appears for dinner in an unsubtle brilliant blue gown "which emphasized the contour of her firmly moulded lower limbs" and has the audacity to compliment Mrs. Villars on her "hostess-gown," which causes her to wince at the popular culture designation, as it is really an old cocktail dress (85-86). Another popular culture target is the radio: throughout *Northbridge Rectory* (205), indeed throughout the oeuvre, various characters criticize the various radio announcers, recoiling at their accents as unacceptable and vilifying their characters. Thirkell often builds on such aesthetic nuances.

37

Another aesthetic difference is pointed up in the long-running joke throughout the book of Miss Crowder's and Miss Hopgood's infatuation with French culture and their misguided attempts to speak French. The name of their cottage (Glycerine) is a ridiculous corruption of the French (Les Glycines), and their mispronounced attempts (pottofur) at other French words (pot au feu) are the source of much quiet humor, as is their great affection for the Pensione Ramsden, which they consider the epitome of French life (49). Additionally, there is a hilarious instance of Miss Hopgood sentimentally referencing children singing a charming little French song, which is in reality a somewhat sophisticated song inappropriate for the young (53).

Dislike and little tolerance are shown toward the refugees who crowd the Northbridge shops, showing no deference to the Rector's wife (114, 120-122). The discussion Mrs. Villars and Miss Pemberton have about the refugees and the lower classes, with reference by Miss Pemberton to Disraeli's *Sybil: The Two Nations*, about the class divide in Victorian England, is a real *cri de coeur* for the passing of the established order. Such regrets for the "Brave New World" will become common in Thirkell's later books, but in *Northbridge Rectory*, published in 1941, the spectre of change is already very apparent.

Although much of Chapter 6 is devoted to descriptions of the rudeness of both the refugees and the lower classes (113-116), one of the most offensive aspects of both is their lack of aesthetic appeal. Thirkell several times uses the word "sham" in describing their fake furs, in addition to focusing on their stoutness, their dyed hair, their painted and dirty fingernails, and their dirty children covered with poultry germs. However, Thirkell, with her usual intelligence, wryly notes that Mrs. Villars then "retired into a nostalgic dream of an age she had never known and many aspects of which she would doubtless have disliked" (122), dreaming of the "Golden Days" of an earlier Bishop, when the clergy and their wives mattered more to society (121).

Marling Hall (1942)

Marling Hall is another wartime novel. In both this book and the one just previous to it, *Northbridge Rectory*, the war is well under way, and, like all of Thirkell's books set in wartime, they concentrate on the home front dealing with the privations of the war. Much of the plot of *Marling Hall* concerns Lettice Watson's nostalgia for married life and her adjustment to her husband's war death at Dunkirk (7). Other characters, like Oliver Marling, adjust to different jobs and, in the case of the Harveys, to dislocation. The Harveys, brother and sister relocated from

London to work in a war office, are often nostalgic for London, particularly Geoffrey, when they are not quarreling between themselves (299). Eventually, after many arguments with his sister, Geoffrey gets his desire and returns to London (305).

There is a lot of difficulty throughout the book in getting farm labor, and Thirkell describes very feelingly the changes that have come to Marling Hall:

> Those [trees] that remain are dying from the head downward in a disconcerting way for want of woodmen ... The small home farm . . . is on its last legs, silent victim of a war which has drained it of its laborers and oppressed it with bureaucracy. . . [I]ts present owner, William Marling . . . sees his small and much loved world crumbling beneath his feet during his life and a fair probability that his family will never be able to live in Marling Hall after his death. . . .
> (5, 7-8)

Some things, however, never change. Despite the fact that male labor is difficult to get, there is still a lot of female household help, and Mrs. Marling asks Miss Harvey with astonishment how she manages with only one maid (106). The older men, too, provide a permanent corps of domestic labor, and the estate still has its own carpenter in Mr. Govern

(298), and the general helper and mechanical genius Ed Pollett, whom Sir Edmund Pridham with real noblesse oblige has got declared unfit for military service because of mental limitations (22).

Another interesting aspect of nostalgia is Mr. Marling's penchant for playing the Old English Squire. His selective deafness and his old-fashioned mode of address to Miss Harvey show his taste for the past (80), as does his opinion of modern poetry:

> "Poetry, eh? Not what it was in my young days. . . . All this modem stuff is what you young men like .... Kipling and A. P. Herbert and that lot. I don't know much about it, the old stuff was good enough for me .... " Lettice [was] amused at her father's rapid progress in his Olde Squire character. . . . (95-96)

Despite all the talk of war, war offices, and soldiers, including wooing by officers and visits from French and colonial enlisted men, some of the greatest wit and aesthetic concern in *Marling Hall* applies to Thirkell's descriptions of modern home decor, specifically Mrs. Smith's Red House. In her many hilarious details throughout the book, Thirkell emphasizes both her interest in beauty (or the lack of beauty) and her opinion of modern taste, especially as practiced by the aspiring middle and lower middle classes. Putting aside the presentation of its light-fingered mistress, The Red House itself has much to dismay the reader, beginning with its outside, an unattractive bastardization of traditional styles with fake accoutrements:

> [The house was] built of a hard purple-red brick . . . the upper story painted with sham timbering . . . The front garden [had] a very small pond edged with synthetic rocks, three dwarfs and a toadstool and a concrete rabbit. (57)

Geoffrey Harvey and David Leslie have an amusing chat about how camp the whole exterior is, with special reference to the dwarves, then they go inside (57-58). It is a draw as to which is worse, the inside or the outside, but Thirkell forges ahead with her devastating description:

> . . . a [table] top painted to imitate marble. . . [In the drawing room] . . . a large reproduction of a picture of bright red horses . . . . a small semicircular table of substitute malachite. . . the dining-room [had] a sham refectory table . . . and chairs with imitation vellum seats. (58-59)

The reiteration of words like sham, synthetic, reproduction, imitation, and substitute, which are the absolute opposite of what the gentry values in decoration, is deadly. With the very careful selection and use of such words, Thirkell is deliberately showing the gulf in the aesthetics of taste between the gentry and the middle and lower middle classes, much as she shows that gulf in literature when Mr. Holden with great glee describes the plot of a typical modem romance novel to Mrs. Villars in *Northbridge Rectory* (276-77)

Growing Up (1943)

The next war book, *Growing Up,* is much less broadly humorous than *Northbridge Rectory* and much more like *Marling Hall* in its exploration of the lives of the young adults affected by the war. The opening ten pages are a charmingly witty description of boys' and men's affection for the Winter Overcotes railway station, and a description of its important passengers, with much nostalgia provided by the stationmaster Mr. Beedle's ruminations on the negative changes in the train system (4-14). There is also the underlying melancholy throughout the book of his son being a prisoner of war (9); the Waring's son's death years earlier but still painful (265-66), and Tommy Needham's loss of his arm, as well as the mysteries of Colin Keith's whereabouts and subsequent posting, Leslie Waring's concern about her brother Cecil, Philip Winter's destination, Sergeant Hopkins's wounding and potential invaliding out, and Noel Merton's and Lydia's individual war assignments, as well as the overall generally unsettled atmosphere provided by the exigencies of war.

With the emphasis on Mr. Beedle's devotion to duty and to the upper classes (he hardly wants to eat when first class carriages are eliminated) (5), Thirkell uses him to express her aesthetic sensibility in regard to the neatness and order of the idealized past. Mr. Beedle often looks back and the very specific contrasts between the past and present are unstintingly described (7-8). Lydia Merton is also appalled by the change in train travel:

> [T]he carriage was full of people who had no business [to be there]. Alien faces, alien languages . . . Cheap tobacco, cheap lipstick, cheap nail-polish, cheap furs, cheap scent characterized the women; a ring on the right hand, pointed unpolished shoes, black-shaven faces distinguished the men. (79)

As seen above, Thirkell is an expert at using elements of material culture to delineate differences in taste and aesthetics. She does it again when she lists the contents of the Warings' stables, one pony and a lot of Victorian artifacts, vividly showing the change in lifestyle at Beliers Priory (105).

Unruly London evacuees come in for their share of opprobrium (9), as does the sly communist Bill Morple (12). But Thirkell, in an acceptance of the times, skillfully describes the female porters in negative aesthetic terms of shiny shirts, tight pants, painted nails, dirty hair, and constant cigarette smoking, while concluding that they were "really very nice, kind girls" (5) and showing often their good humor and helpfulness, uncowed as they are by authority or formality (13-14).

The ongoing negative remarks about the appearance of Beliers Priory are reminiscent of those about Pomfret Towers in that eponymous book. Thirkell has a wonderful grasp of architecture and architectural history, and she is especially caustic about the excesses of the Victorian age. Elsewhere she notes the horror of the chapel at Southbridge School, she has Lady Cora Palliser deride her family's Victorian pile, she has a very lengthy and hilarious description of Brandon Abbey, and here in *Growing Up*, she delightedly details the bad design of Beliers Priory, which "combined inconvenience and discomfort in the highest form" (15). For example, it rains in the hall, the corridors and the rooms are dark, and the bathrooms impossible (15).

But it is not only the upper class houses that are mocked for bad architecture: Ladysmith Cottages, rented to old servants of Beliers Priory, are well built but aesthetically unappealing (47).   By contrast, Jasper Margett's cottage is incredibly picturesque but "suffered from every drawback of picturesque rural life," including dimness, flooding, dry well, drafts, and bad odors (110-11). Nature is heralded in the setting of Jasper's cottage, and in the lyrical descriptions of Golden Valley's "green mistiness" and "early wild flowers" (322).

The personal descriptions of Jasper include his "autumn leaf coloured coat, breeches and leggings" and his ever-present gun, as well as his superstitions and his deliberately bucolic manner of speech. Another of the most memorable aesthetic personal descriptions in this book is again not of a main character (those physical descriptions are very sketchy) but of Selena Crockett, the servant whose pretty plumpness, curly silvering hair, and tendency to cry are used to delineate her kindly character (16-18). Selena, approaching fifty, is a gentle soul who is bossed not only by her employer but by her mother and by the school matron (16). Ultimately, even her marriage is arranged for her, after the gentry deciding among themselves that Jasper the Gypsy keeper is unsuitable (271, 323, 327).

Finally, *Growing Up* contains three of the most unromantic romances ever detailed, even by Thirkell. Tommy Needham, engaged to marry Octavia Crawley through the earlier efforts of Lydia Keith, leaves it to Lydia Merton to help secure Sir Harry's parsonage for him (289-293) and suggest they get on with the marriage (288); Lydia Merton lets her husband know she is pregnant through a discussion of what is allowed of patriots (340); and Philip Winter becomes engaged to Leslie Waring with a ring he used on Rose Birkett, and that only through the efforts of Lydia Merton, who says to Leslie that the ring "is yours if you want it" (325). As a romantic proposal, this latter is rivaled only by Geoff Fairweather's off-handed proposal to Geraldine Birkett at the end of *Cheerfulness Breaks In*.

The Headmistress (1944)

The Headmistress opens with a delightful description of the village of Harefield, its River Rising, Harefield Park, and a brief history of the Belton family (3-4), with a later description of the charm of the village and its usual pretty, arched bridge (125). As usual, there is much attention to the beauties of architecture: Harefield Park is a "plain-faced Palladian house which stands connected by a covered arcade with a pavilion on each side," (3) and has "finely decorated ceilings" (20), while Plassey House has a "beautiful carved shell-shaped projection over the front door" and a large garden with an historic tree (56). Dowlah Cottage is "quite a commodious little home with a wide hall running from front to back, four rooms downstairs and four up" (170).

Arcot House, which the elder Beltons move into after letting the Park to a school, is a "small but handsome house in the village . . . [with] white walls [and] good furniture" (5). Further, there is a charming description of the clutter in the attics, evoking the Victorian past (121-24), as does the description of particularly attractive old-fashioned jewelry (181-83). Particularly nice is the Garden House at Harefield, a "cottage orné with a pagoda roof . . . a very small artificial lake . . . and a Palladian covered bridge," but now sadly fallen on hard times (119-120). Harefield Church, "almost a small cathedral" is also notable with "its handsome square tower" and "melodious" bells (114).

Thirkell is also just as enamoured as ever of nature, describing a sunset and elsewhere having Elsa Belton and Christopher Hornby admire the view of the valley, the river, and the church from the bridge (126). Later, the two of them see two hundred airplanes "looking as light as silver feathers in the frosty blue," and Christopher Hornby laments "the end of peace and quiet to have the sky full of noise" (262).

The book continues the theme of the home front in war, emphasizing the evacuation of a London girls' school led by Miss Sparling, the only admirable scholarly female in Thirkell's oeuvre, and it is in this book that the rank outsider, the badly dressed, ungrammatical, brashly spoken, extremely wealthy Sam Adams makes his first appearance. Mr. Adams improves greatly over the years, and Thirkell says of him that "I became very fond of Mr. Adams too . . . he literally raised himself by his own exertions and his general probity" (quoted in Strickland 152). Mr. Adams, however, is not so propitious when he is first introduced in his brashly coloured tweeds, yellow shirt, and blue sweater and tie, to say nothing of his hairy hands (225).

In Mrs. Belton's conversation with him, she is quite put off by his manner of introducing himself (234-35). He talks too much (284-85), exhausting his listeners, and is very self-satisfied, but even in this first book, Mr. Adams has some redeeming qualities, which qualities will grow in later books: he is a doting father, he is grateful for kindness to his daughter, he is helpful whenever he can be, he is patriotic, and he is efficient. As he improves over the years, his dress and speech both become more aesthetically pleasing, a sign of his growing acceptance by the county.

Another interesting aesthetic element lies in the description of Charles Belton, appearing on leave in a "gigantic and dirty raincoat . . . a very tight pale green beret," of which his mother thinks, but does not say, "What a hideous colour, darling, and your face looks just like a pudding boiled in a cloth under it"

(21).   Further, his bedroom is very quickly "strewn with equipment" and junk (29). That and his deliberate lateness help to further limn the young Charles. Thirkell is not so much interested in what Charles actually looks like as she is in establishing his rather gauche behavior, and in exploring, which she does very delicately, the awkward relationship between humorously craven parents and bumptious grown child (20-28).   In later books, he, like Sam Adams, improves greatly. Other personal description relates to Miss Sparling's deliberate schoolteacher "disguise," as even she thinks of it (230), as differing from the standard county female attire of tweed coat and skirt (140-41), and to the "Robin Hood" hats and unattractive clothing of Miss Pettinger and Dr. Morgan (230-232, 274).

In *The Headmistress*, there are several mentions of "the Raeburn," an apparent reference to a portrait by Sir Henry Raeburn, the Scottish painter of the late eighteenth and early nineteenth centuries, but there are indications that he is not seen as a great artist, in that there are multiple mentions of the highlight on the end of the nose that is apparently a hallmark of most of his portraits and in the same book, Sir Cecil Waring gently cleans a painting belonging to Mrs. Hoare, but more from reasons of curiosity than love of art, and the painting is revealed as only an apparently anonymous still life, with little else said about it.

Interestingly, *The Headmistress* has very little reminiscing about events of the former books, although throughout the novel various characters do catch each other up on events in the lives of relatives and acquaintances. Rather, the elements of nostalgia, perhaps best expressed by Mrs. Belton at different times, are for a kinder, gentler past, an understandable emotion in the fifth year of war.

Miss Bunting (1945)

Miss Bunting is the sixth World War II book. It is something of a sidebar, focusing as it does on the maturing of Anne Fielding and on her relationship with her revered governess, Miss Bunting. However, war elements run through the book, and the two most poignant are Miss Bunting's ongoing dream of saving the world in general and her students in particular from Hitler, a goal that is finally achieved in her mind at her death (283), and Jane Gresham's ongoing worry and wonder about her missing husband, a question that is finally resolved to her relief as the book ends (288, 294).

Miss Bunting opens with the familiar device of Thirkell describing the idyllic setting of the town, in this case Hallbury (1-2), with an explanation of the gap between the Old Town and the New Town, a gap that is solidified by most of the gentry living in the former (2, 6-7), and most of the upstarts in the latter. Naturally, the architecture reflects the aesthetic taste of the two groups, such that the Old Town's church is "one of the many beautiful and unpretentious stone churches of these parts" (10), with accompanying rectory and charming stable (11).

By contrast, the house in which Mrs. Merivale rents rooms to Mr. Adams and his daughter for the summer is a tract house of no particular distinction (16). In a kind of reprise of the descriptions of Joyce Smith's house that she rents to the Harveys in Marling Hall, Thirkell has a lot of fun with the decoration of Mrs. Merivale's house. The "lounge" has "hideous elephantine chairs," a bookcase with only magazines, a few ill-hung watercolors, and "a flight of wild ducks in china . . . with a bulgy side for the public and a flat side which only the wall could see. . . ." (16). Jane's response is "May I say how much I was struck by those flying ducks. I have never seen anything like them before," a not unqualified compliment, but Mrs. Merivale is pleased (17). Jane further compliments "the little green china hearts let into the back of the sideboard," while admiring the fumed oak dining room furniture, all elements never to be found in the houses of people with good aesthetic taste (17). It is also in this passage that the first reference to the "lodger" appears (17), a running joke which is shown by book's end to be Mrs. Merivale's interpretation of the "loggia" (267).

Jane Gresham feels a reciprocated quiet attraction to Mr. Adams, but, with her delicate taste, she is put off by aesthetic elements of his loud clothes and hairy hands (275), and the fact that "Mr. Adams was not of her class . . . Mr. Adams . . . was not a gentleman and never would be" (266-67), not something that will later bother Lucy Marling, with her sturdy fair-mindedness. There are even more fine shades of class feeling in this book, as Lady Fielding is forced into unwilling acquaintance with the upstart Sam Adams and his daughter (86-87). "She did not dislike Mr. Adams and found Heather inoffensive, but the feeling of wealth, the extravagant presents, made her uneasy" (246). Lady Fielding, of course, has both a town and a country house, as well as servants for both and a governess for her daughter, so her distaste for wealth, in Mr. Adams' case earned by his own efforts, is a bit disingenuous.

One aesthetic element that turns up from time to time in various books, first mentioned in *High Rising* as noted earlier, is the beauty of the traditional Anglican service. Much loved as Dr. Dale is by his congregation, Thirkell notes that one reason is that "[H]e had stuck to the old forms," and she goes on to give a lengthy disquisition about the services, the hymns, the psalms, etc. (131). True to Thirkell forms, any change is anathema and traditional is best, a position that becomes ever more entrenched as time marches on, and one that may be a result of aging and/or of resisting unwanted social and political change. An excellent discussion of Britain in this post-war Labour government period, *Austerity Britain*, makes Thirkell's resistance all too understandable (Kynaston). That traditional Anglican service controls Jane Gresham's mood, as she gets lost in its comfort, then is rudely awakened to again face the terrible ambiguity of her husband's POW status (142).

Throughout, Jane seems strangely ambivalent, as instanced above, about what she wishes to have happened to her husband, rumored to be a prisoner of war, but that ambivalence may be a result of the common knowledge of the harsh treatment of prisoners by the Japanese, and of her wanting to spare him agony, but she also seems torn, perhaps understandably, by the question of what their relationship will be like if and when he returns after such a long separation.

In the meantime, there are hilarious nasty accounts of modern reviewers who have been unkind to Mrs. Morland (read Mrs. Thirkell) (71) and lots of opportunities for typical wartime nostalgia for the past (70). The other element of nostalgia is the passing of Miss Bunting and the fading of Dr. Dale. Miss Bunting's death is handled very delicately

(282-83), and will be the vehicle for bringing together Anne Fielding and David Leslie later in *Peace Breaks Out*. Here, that death and Dr. Dale's gradual withdrawal as he approaches death, bring together Robin and Anne, who turn to each other with growing affection (280-82, 294-95).

Peace Breaks Out (1946)

Peace Breaks Out is the last World War II book and the single book for which Thirkell has gotten the most virulently negative reaction, due to having her characters belittle the peace and seemingly long for the war to continue, although she uses this device in several future books, where it is not as shocking since it is not as close to war's end. Her dislike of sentimentality seems to be one element of attributing such ideas to her characters, as she does not support the standard view of cheering the end of the war without thought of what is to come. This idiosyncratic approach seems to be based mostly on her dislike of and dismay at the election of the Labour government, and, of course, she is, as usual, enmeshed in nostalgia, in this case nostalgia for people pulling together, working for a common cause, and overcoming petty differences as they work to win the war and save England. The fact that that has happened, but England has greatly changed, due to the new government, means her joy in the victory, which for her in some ways has turned to ashes, is diminished, shown by the thoughts of Lady Fielding, as she longs for "Peace. Golden peace, not the pinchbeck that was being offered, indeed thrust upon people, in its place" (130). Peace is awkwardly announced in the middle of the night (257-59), to everyone's great inconvenience, and Thirkell also very clearly shows, both near the beginning of the book and at various points throughout, how worn down, tired, and depressed everyone is by the six years of war, making them less receptive of and grateful for even good change (6, 13, 63, 68-69, 78, 98-99).

Additionally, Thirkell was one of the first writers, since her books are written in real time, to acknowledge the effect of the war on young people, even those who had successfully come through it, For the next several books, as there is here for the Halliday brother and sister, there will be the theme of young people somewhat lost as they are set adrift from wartime accomplishment to finding peacetime places for themselves in the new society. Sylvia Halliday "thought a little wistfully of her W. A. A. F., for now that her days in it were about to be numbered . . . all began to assume a nostalgic rose-colour" (145).

This theme will grow in later books to focus on the struggles of Tom Grantly, Lady Cora Palliser, Isabel Dale, Lord Silverbridge, and many others, to adapt to the post-war world and will have such disparate characters as Mr. Adams and Mrs. Belton reflecting with great sensitivity and compassion on how difficult it is for the younger people to adapt to the "Brave New World" after the war with no set direction for them and with the difficulty of finding a place for themselves in that world. The older people don't struggle to such an extent, as they have known a world between the wars, so are able to revert to normalcy, except for Them. David Leslie, fortyish, is old enough to have a foot in both worlds, and regrets that most young people won't remember the niceties of the "murdered civilization" (95-96).

Interestingly, Thirkell in *Peace Breaks Out* uses the naivete of Anne Fielding to show the conventional view, as Anne is horrified at the Hallidays' complaining about the war being over, a device that should have mollified the critics. But George and Sylvia Halliday, brother and sister, have grown to young adulthood in a society with one aim, and now that that aim is achieved, or partially so, since the book begins just as the European peace is about to be announced and ends just after the Pacific one, they are feeling extraneous and confused, as well as cross (15). Thirkell's sophistication in being so quick to explore this issue is not appreciated by some of her critics, who would apparently have preferred that she simply cheerlead for the victory. It is also interesting that she is so uncritically patriotic about the monarchy, for example, but much more critical about the peace, again, probably due to her reservations about the new government, as well as to her dislike of sentimentality, a stance that often has her expressing negative remarks about children (despite her frequent positive gushing about their appearance), Christmas, and other icons, so her remarks about the war ending should be taken as further establishing her curmudgeon credentials and not as ill-wishing or unpatriotic.

Peace Breaks Out opens with the familiar aesthetic device of a delightful description of the village of Hatch End, the River Rising, and Hatch House, along with some sidebars about Mr. Scatcherd the artist, the usual inconvenient railway station, and Sir Ogilvy Hibberd (5-7). There is a stark contrast between Thirkell's lyrical description of earlier springs and her grim description of the current situation, a use of the pathetic fallacy that will appear again and again in the postwar books:

> Today, when a war against the powers of darkness was well into its sixth year, when the older people were living valiantly with tiredness and even hopelessness as their constant companions, when even the young were wondering if anything really mattered or if one might as well gamble away all one had, a chill spring wind was battering the

reeds along the water channels and turning the leaves of the aspens till everything looked as grey as steel, and even the waters were wrinkled with cold, while depressed cows stood with their patient backs to the blast and chewed without enthusiasm. (13)

The Hallidays are so depressed they engage in chat and socialization with the banally traditional and untalented working class artist Mr. Scatcherd, allowing Thirkell the joyful opportunity of describing his house in all its horrible glory of bad proportions, dark interior, and ugly raw bricks (18). By contrast, Number Seventeen, the Fieldings' house in the Close, has wide curved steps, a beautiful shell projection over the front door, and "the most exquisite spiral staircase in the county [which] wound upwards with harmonious curve " (44).

Rushwater, which will later be so admired, is described here in its "complacent comfortable ugliness" (90), while its inhabitants in Anne Fielding's eyes, are all remarkable for their size (92). Mr. Macpherson's Regency house is charming and delightful and "too good for the agent," being as it is better suited for Emmy Graham (192).

Despite her description of the depressing spring weather, Thirkell also includes her usual aesthetically pleasing descriptions of the English countryside, the twilight, and later some cooperative weather (71, 100, 154, 184, 190-91, 201), as well as David Leslie's aesthetic appreciation of the music of Anne's singing voice: "[A] bird's soft effortless notes rose on wings . . . David, too susceptible to beauty . . . waited in almost unbearable suspense for the next verse. The small miracle was repeated" (78).

There are a number of personal descriptions: Sylvia Halliday is repeatedly referred to as a "Winged Victory," with special reference to her "goldenness" (220) and Anne Fielding's elegance and slimness are often cited. Less auspicious is the unattractive description of Miss Banks, hired due to the shortage of masters to fill a position at Southbridge School, humiliated whenever possible, and fired soon after the war ends (161). There is a lot of byplay about the pronunciation of "Uranus," which seems much ado about nothing until one realizes that Miss Banks' pronunciation as "Uraynus" translates as "yer anus," an old English schoolboy joke, hence everyone's horror at Leslie Major's deliberate repetition of it (165-69) (Moor).

Nostalgia certainly makes its appearance throughout, and is especially notable in Anne Fielding's and Clarissa Graham's discussions of Miss Bunting (227-228) and David Leslie's remembrances of the summer of *Wild Strawberries* (221). The nostalgia is deliberately banal as David recounts a boring story about his childhood but has "an uneasy feeling that no one really cared" (233). Finally, this is the book in which, after mentions throughout of David's flirtatious past and of his unsettled future, Rose Bingham firmly tells him they will be married (244).

CHAPTER IV: POST WAR 1946-1951

It is really in the post-war novels that Thirkell's aesthetic appreciation and nostalgic feeling reach a crescendo. The first three, *Private Enterprise, Love Among the Ruins,* and *The Old Bank House,* published respectively in 1947, 1948, and 1949 all have strong elements of each.

Private Enterprise (1947)

As in *Marling Hall*, Thirkell describes in *Private Enterprise* (1947) a house that is rented by people displaced by the war. Although the Arbuthnots, sisters-in-law, have very little money, they are clearly gentry, and most of their efforts at decorating involve undoing efforts of the previous tenant and imposing their own much plainer taste. When they first see the house they will rent, it is notable for its decoration, and heavy curtains, such that "it was hardly to be believed" (48).

Noel Merton, however, reacts to the house, Editha Cottage, as did Geoffrey Harvey and David Leslie to the Red House, essentially saying it is so awful that Colin's friends must indeed rent it (46). Where the upper classes would value the aesthetics of light, space, and order, others value machine made, often imitation, goods. One very telling element in its description is the presence of only one bookcase, despite the fullness of the house, and that bookcase a hanging one; the gentry read, so they need bookcases, and the Arbuthnots have several minor arguments with workmen about the bookcases for the house (138).

Thirkell combines her love of nostalgia with her love of the aesthetics of nature in Mrs. Brandon's musings about nature reflecting the dreary experiences of the past few years, as she is driven through the countryside, a throwback to Thirkell's descriptions of nature years earlier in *The Brandons*:

> As they drove in that horrid damp chilly afternoon which was all that the summer could manage, Mrs. Brandon's thoughts went back to summers before the war when the sun had shone and the wind had been still and the rich, green Barsetshire country had lain warm and peaceful in the golden tight. Now everything was grey, an uneasy wind ruffled every leaf, every blade, every stream and pond, and Mrs. Brandon felt chilly and old. (*Private Enterprise* 185-86)

Mr. Birkett goes a bit farther in drawing the comparison:

> Now we've got this wretched peace, we shan't have any more frosts, I suppose.

Look at the weather this Government has brought on us. No summer and no proper winter. Just one long run of nasty chilly wet weather. Why we were ever born I don't know. (51)

Mr. Birkett, like Mrs. Brandon, is reflecting the human belief in the pathetic fallacy, the idea that nature reflects human emotions, even more emphatically expressed when the Deans decide to give a tennis party: "The weather, inspired thereto perhaps by the state of affairs it saw going on all over England, was outdoing itself in nastiness" (92).

In truth, Mrs. Brandon is indeed older, so it is not surprising that she and Mr. Birkett should feel older and, after living through the war, should be more discouraged. She, formerly an icon of serenity, has been psychologically hard hit by the general malaise. She expresses the feelings of many in her thoughts about the Labour government, that the populace was "battered for the last year by discomfort and tyranny beyond what they had yet felt, mostly inflicted upon them by their own countrymen, feeling, when they allowed themselves to think, very hopeless about the future. . . . " (92).

Private Enterprise, the first post-war book, also contains many, many references by the various characters to past books, with Lydia Merton and Nanny Twicker recalling the summer of *Summer Half* (3-4, 133-34, 150-151), Nurse and Susan Dean recalling the events of *August Folly* (10,35,97), Sir Edmund Pridham, Francis Brandon, and Mrs. Brandon reminiscing about happenings from *The Brandons* (33, 41, 381). Noel Merton discusses the same summers of *Summer Half* and *The Brandons* (21, 43, 65), Everard Carter also remembers the time periods of *Summer Half*(50-51, 303) and *Cheerfulness Breaks In* (78,270), and the Birketts and Brandons discuss the incidents from *Cheerfulness Breaks In* (255).

It is easy to see that Thirkell, while perhaps needing some of this expiation for plot clarification purposes, is also indulging her penchant for wallowing in nostalgia, especially in the face of the so-called "Brave New World." One of her characters' particular hardships to bear is the ongoing post-war rationing, and Thirkell is harsh and funny at the same time about it throughout the book, as in the passage about the irritations and difficulties of changing Bread Units for food points, to say nothing of the futility, because of the unavailability of any food one might want (310).

Love Among the Ruins (1948)

Love Among the Ruins has many of the same elements of aesthetics and nostalgia as does *Private Enterprise*. *Love Among the Ruins* is one of Thirkell's longest books and considered by some critics to be too sprawling and repetitive. One could view it instead as incredibly rich and encompassing. There are many instances of nostalgia and many of aesthetics, and a large number of examples of the two are mingled.

As in *Private Enterprise, Love Among the Ruins* contains a myriad of nostalgic references by its characters to the events of past books. Lady Waring and Philip Winter remind people of events from *Growing Up* (7, 299), Martin Leslie and Lady Agnes Graham talk at different times about the summer from *Wild Strawberries* (151 and 307, 328-29 and 340 and 364), as does Clarissa Graham (337). Gradka Bonescu reminds a group of diners of the year of *Miss Bunting* (236) and the Deans and Tebbens discuss their past experiences in *August Folly* (386, 68). Richard Tebben also recalls that period (99) and Emmy Leslie remembers Lucy Marling teaching her to wring a chicken's neck from *Marling Hall* (129).

In regard to aesthetics, Thirkell continues to idealize the English landscape, as in a description of Rushwater with its polished floors and windows, its beautiful curtains with their handsome rods, its Chinese vase full of branches and flowers, and its lovely view of the lawn and the woods (333-334).

Emmy Leslie and Lucy Marling marvel at the golden sunlight and the peacefulness (130), as does Clarissa Graham (135). Lucy Marling realizes how idealized the whole scene is at Rushwater, and it causes her to wonder what actually will happen in the future at her own old home, Marling Hall: "[I]t was probably the end. . . . She saw Marling under a grey sky, all the old world tumbling down and no new world to replace it (132)."

Freddy Belton thinks of his old home as Lucy does of hers:

> [A]s the strange magic twilight deepened he came down from the hills wondering as he went what the fate of Harefield would be .... no help could more than stave off the evil day during his father's lifetime, after which he and Charles would probably be homeless. (189)

Finally, Thirkell combines the sense of beauty and the sense of loss in a passage about Barchester, seen through the eyes of Mrs. Belton. She hears the Cathedral bells, and goes in the lovely Close with its beautiful houses. There she sees an old gardener cutting the grass with a pony wearing slippers, and she tears up as she realizes such scenes will be lost in the future, as so much that is familiar and beautiful is also gone (165-66). Lady Fielding comes up to her and they lament "the land of lost content" (166).

Interestingly, *Love Among the Ruins* also contains a passage in which the face of the future, Mr. Adams, proclaims his political independence and excoriates both parties, and the face of past nostalgia, Mr. Belton, admits the conservatives have little to offer as a political program, so for once Thirkell is less antagonistic in her politics than is usual for her (430).

The Old Bank House (1949)

The Old Bank House is a favorite of many readers, perhaps because of its beautiful architectural aesthetics and good cheer about the future. While filled with hilarious passages about Doris and Edna Thatcher and their "Children of Shame" (102-03), a long-standing Thirkell term for children born out of wedlock, this book looks sturdily toward the future, including a vision of change in society as people like Sam Adams and his daughter and unseen son-in-law are given credit for their contributions. The Grantlys, who are "county," actually look forward to having Mr. Adams as a neighbor, despite his rough edges. The novel is full of the usual fussing about "Them," even on the part of the Thatchers (102-03) and even as the Thatchers show the supposedly lower class desire to get something for nothing and so abuse the national health system (138-39), but overall the tone is quite light and the nostalgia less present than in the previous book, despite the fact that the Labour government is still in power.

The Old Bank House itself is almost revered, and the handover from Miss Sowerby to Mr. Adams is by way of being a passing of the torch from the old way of life to the new. Miss Sowerby knows the full value of what she has (54), as does Sam Adams, who promises to love and respect the beautiful house and its elegant furniture. Thirkell revels in the descriptions of this house Miss Sowerby sells: like the Fieldings' house in the Close, the Old Bank House has a shell canopy over the door. It has beautifully proportioned windows, a wide hall and a perfect staircase, and lovely period furniture, along with the much-admired faded Chinese wallpaper (22-23).

Even more charming is the description of the house when Sam Adams holds his open house after refurbishing:

> The long drawing-room newly hung with the Chinese paper, the Chinese-Chippendale sofa conscious of its elegance, the curtains of pre-war silk ... the gilded mirrors, its sole ornament two or three immense Chinese vases with flowers rising from them . . . . [T]he dining-room with its silver-striped paper and severe mahogany with some good

69

silver and crystal; the noble staircase newly painted and carpeted . . . . (209)

County Chronicle (1950)

By contrast, *County Chronicle*, published in 1950 when English society was still trying to adjust to the world after the war, has a much more melancholic strain running through it than do most of the Barsetshire books. The twin themes of Isabel Dale and Lady Cora Palliser mourning their lost loves, killed in the war, come up repeatedly and nostalgically as both ladies, twenty-nine and thirty respectively, try to cope with a somewhat bleak future. The sadness and nostalgia come to a poignant crescendo with Lady Cora's singing of "Keep the Home Fires Burning" at the Conservative "do" at Gatherum Castle, and not just Isabel and Lady Cora, but most of the audience, represented in particular by the Leslies thinking of their son Giles, are brought to the brink of tears by a wave of sadness and nostalgia, such that Lady Cora tells her brother the next day that she never should have sung that song and that it is devastating to look back (339). Dr. Joram understands her pain, and he feels "compassionate admiration for these gallant supporters of a dying civilization living so often behind a mask of flippancy" (258).

Similarly, Lord Silverbridge is writing a history of the Barsetshire military in World War II, and there is, unusually for Thirkell, a great deal of war detail about the various landings, the fighting in Italy, and the specifics of the death of Isabel Dale's fiancée John. Both Mr. Wickham and Lord Silverbridge are shown to have been in active fighting, and both several times comfort Isabel about the quickness of John's death in action, but such great detail about a relatively recent death gives this book a much more somber flavor than do recollections of other deaths such as those of John Leslie's wife and Freddie Belton's Wren.

As an aside, *County Chronicle* has the various characters showing just a little too much interest in Isabel Dale's financial status to make the modern reader comfortable. Mr. Wickham, Oliver Marling, and Lord Silverbridge all propose to her after hearing of her inheritance, although Mr. Wickham is known for his pity proposals, and the latter two do have the grace to recognize that the money makes their proposals awkward. Nevertheless, they push ahead, with an imperative not felt before the news, and Lord Silverbridge, who wins the lady's hand, even announces the engagement to his parents by saying first that now he can run for Parliament (336).

Despite the melancholic strain, *County Chronicle* is, like all the Barsetshire books, basically a comedic novel of manners, and contains many passages of aesthetic appreciation. The altar cloth that Mrs. Brandon embroiders with "pre-war silks" is greatly admired (224), as is the lusciously-described shawl that Jessica gives Lucy Marling before her marriage, right down to the envious reactions of the various females present (35). Jessica notes that she brought it back from the United States, and it is, of course, a special treat in the general sparseness of post-war Britain. That sparseness is also shown in many passages about how pinched life is, such as the explanation of (Summer Time, few servants, not enough heating oil, and too much after dinner work) and regret for the passing of the custom of dressing for dinner in "pretty frocks" and dinner jackets (61-62). Perhaps because of such general sparseness, pretty bags supplied by Mr. Adams for Lucy Marling's bridesmaids, come as a delightful treat and are lovingly described (75), as is the outfit Jessica wears to the wedding "a cloud of black lace with a twenty-five guinea piece of nonsense on her head that no one else could have worn" (89). Aesthetic details of Lucy Marling's wedding preparations are charmingly reported, with humor about her resistance to ornament and to her feeling "like a cow at a cattle show with ribbons on her" (83-87).

Houses here garner their share of admiration. The Marlings' drawing room has a "handsome cornice and paneling, [and] its long line of French windows on three sides" (51), and the bedroom Mrs. Marling assigns Isabel "faced west and was drenched in warm sunlight. The old-fashioned wallpaper of large pink roses . . . the good walnut furniture . . . an embroidered bell-pull" and an array of old books and bits of china give the flavor of a family home (58). Dr. Joram's house in the Close has similar "dignified white paneling and the good, old-fashioned furniture" (109), but the notable thing about his house is the staircase painting of gods and goddesses that elicits gasps of admiration from his visitors (108).

A house that is not so admired is Gatherum Castle, which is compared to Euston Station (237). It is "so huge, so hideous, so inconvenient that to dispose of it was impossible," and there is no money for upkeep so the National Trust won't take it. "It had for many years been the bane and almost the ruin of its owners" (237). But they get lucky and it is leased by a government office, so the family goes into the servant's quarters, as did the family at Pomfret Towers (238). A saving grace is a portion of the grounds, which "gave Oliver [Marling] so astounding a shock of romance and hidden beauty that he was quite incapable of words" (243). Other delightful gardens are the Deanery garden (97), as well as the Bishop's beautiful garden (162).

Barchester Cathedral has Mrs. Morland "overcome by the beauty of the great white nave drenched in afternoon sunlight" (105). Like many of Thirkell's descriptions of either natural or architectural beauty, here she sets the stage with natural light, and there is much mention of sitting on the lawn in the evening under the Spanish chestnut tree (226) at Stories. Similarly, Thirkell says of the Great House at Allington that "In the late afternoon sunlight the lovely yellow-grey stone . . . was pure gold" (298), although both Isabel Dale and Robin Dale loathe it, apparently because of its association with her disliked mother (317). By contrast, the Victorian School Chapel at Southbridge, where Anne and Robin Dale's babies are christened, "combined darkness and inconvenience in an unparalleled degree, not to speak of the hideous east window . . .[and] the pitch-pine paneling" (134). Another public arena is highlighted with the very long-winded, precise, and witty description of Market Day in Barsetshire running into the Bishop's Garden Party (161).

Personal description in this book is mostly focused on Isabel Dale, who is described with much more physical detail than are most of the other characters (316): she is "tall, good-looking, fair, and blue-eyed with the oval face that is to-day very rare . . . . [T]hough her lips were slightly reddened her nails were not" (55), the latter showing her good taste and upper class status. Other characters are delineated through descriptions of their clothing: Miss Bent wears "a very full ankle-length skirt of printed cotton, a floppy Mixo-Lydian blouse embroidered in red and blue and a halo hat of shiny red straw, the whole embellished with six coral necklaces" (146), a description similar to that of Mrs. Grant (164), while Rose Fairweather wears a New Look dress of "ravishing elegance and simplicity," as well as gorgeous shoes, hair and make-up (148). Mrs. Brandon is several times reminded by Dr. Joram of how pretty she looked in her "sweet pea" dress early in the war (172), and Mrs. Brandon has another evocative description, that of a perfect little tray dinner served in bed at the end of an exhausting day (198-199).

As *County Chronicle* draws to a close, the nostalgia theme is again raised, this time in a more cheerful manner, with a description of a bazaar including Mr. Packer's Universal Royal Derby, giving various attendees a chance to mentally reminisce (313).

The Duke's Daughter (1951)

In *The Duke's Daughter*, Thirkell turns her attention to a very different set of Barsetshire families. Although the book opens with attention to Lucy Adams and further descriptions of the Old Bank House (9, 21), and Heather Adams has, surprisingly, become a "tall good-looking young woman" (10), the real attention is on Tom Grantly and Lady Cora

Palliser, the eponymous duke's daughter first introduced in *County Chronicle*. Thirkell gives a very sensitive treatment to the problems of the unsettled young discomposed by the war years (120), although at twenty-eight and thirty, respectively, they are not still so young. Thirkell writes knowingly of the "terrible malaise" that precludes "any settled life" and has "taken the savour from living" (16). Thirkell also admits the great gulf between those who saw war action and those who didn't, and she very poignantly highlights Mrs. Grantly's feeling about not being able to know what her son Tom has been through during the war and how it has affected him, extrapolated by her (16) and later by Sam Adams (20) to encompass others in his situation. Similarly, his father notes that Tom is restless working at Rushwater (20), a foreshadowing of his career change, over which he has much angst, then and in the future. He is especially torn when he leaves the Red Tape and Sealing Wax office after just a few months to return to his real love of farming at Rushwater, where Martin Leslie, an ex-soldier himself, is very sympathetic (120-21).

Tom Grantly is the first concern, as his mother and Lucy Adams early on discuss his feelings and his future (16). Although the books are filled with various office workers who are certainly well-respected, such as Oliver Marling and Mr. Tebben, most of the characters in *The Duke's Daughter* seem to feel that Tom is best served being an agricultural labourer, a plan that in the long run works out for him as he gains a wife, and therefore a house, on the Rushwater estate, but it is a long and uncomfortable road for him as he finds his way. If he had not married Emmy Graham, one wonders what his future would have been, as, although he is Oxford-educated, with a decent second, and he has a real feel for the land and the animals, he has difficulty with the paperwork required of an agent (97). One element that, of course, tips the balance in favor of the agricultural life is that his office superior is the much-hated Geoffrey Harvey, which fact causes Tom's bureaucratic career to become less and less appealing.

Lady Cora Palliser's multiple references to her aesthetically pleasing legs are clearly "whistling in the wind," a way to cheer herself since all her young men were killed in the war (96). Although she was not engaged to him, one "Froggy," an impecunious younger son with an eye for the ladies, features often in her nostalgic speech. A similar element of nostalgia also shows in the description of Lady Waring's musings on death, as she regrets again the loss of her son, killed in World War I, and the more recent loss of her husband (57).

But Lady Cora, who has done yeoman war service driving a general (during which time she met Wickham in London during an air raid), is at loose ends with a bleak future, and although she kindly takes an interest in her brother's and Isabel Dale's house hunt and is very helpful in getting Sir Cecil Waring to lease The Lodge to them, she feels that life has passed her by and left her stranded with little prospect of marriage or children, and no need for her wartime driving skills. Sir Cecil, in looking at the women, Lady Cora and Isabel, is struck by the beauty of the two English roses (102).

Sir Cecil Waring, older than either Tom or Lady Cora, is also the most stable of the three, heir as he is to Beliers Priory, with his path of duty clearly marked. Additionally, he has his own philanthropic plans for a boys school, seemingly a default vocation, as Philip Winter, founder of yet another school, brings in Charles Belton and Eric Swan, both of whom are at loose ends after the war (70). Sir Cecil is very like Elsa Belton's husband Christopher Hornby, not only in his brisk competence, but in that he has had a distinguished military career despite being heir to a great estate.

Charles Belton, too, having served in the war, is shown to be somewhat adrift in this and later books, as he cannot seem to move forward with his marriage to Clarissa Graham. But, nostalgic as he is for his family's more prosperous past, and appreciative as he is of the beauties of Harefield House, his placid nature has him following the path of least resistance in going to work as a schoolmaster for Philip Winter; Charles' association with Philip's school will eventually let Charles live at Harefield House, albeit as a staff member. It is

Charles' plan to cut rushes on the lake that drives the central romance of this book (58).

Lord Lufton also has served in the war, and is marking time at home with his mother, running the estate and waiting for his life to move forward, i.e. waiting to grow up some more and get married. He is living in rather straitened circumstances, boarding with a miserly cousin when he is in London for the House of Lords. His sense of tradition helps promote his attraction to Grace Grantly, as he is so enthralled by her beauty and dignity in his mother's ceremonial robes

In the only reference to fine art here, the Duke of Omnium suggests that Isabel Dale, married to his son Lord Silverbridge, "should have some Canalettos for the long drawing room, to which she did not say no" (105), leading one to ponder whether he could have raised the money himself for his son to run for Parliament by selling off a painting or two, rather than using part of Isabel Dale's fortune.

The usual negative aesthetic remarks are made about the hideousness of both Gatherum Castle (155-56) and Beliers Priory (77, 146-49), as Lady Cora and Sir Cecil respectively compete for the honor of the ugliest house. Conversely, the glory of beautiful architecture is spotlighted in loving descriptions of various other houses. Mr. Macpherson's little Regency house is elegant with all its very appropriate ornament (54). Dowlah Cottage, the home of

Freddy Belton and his wife Susan Dean, is delightful with its wide passage and its pleasant garden (56). Plassey House's "beautifully carved shell-shaped projection over the front door" and its big cedar tree come in for admiration (61), as does the outdoor setting of Rushwater (131, 134, 140-42).

The most aesthetically pleasing descriptions are of The Lodge, Sir Cecil Waring's house in Silverbridge, symbolizing the beautiful past as narrated by Mr.Winthrop (89-92), and of The Cedars, the house Mr. Marling gives to his son Oliver. Silverbridge itself is presented as a lovely town, as yet unspoiled by chain stores (88), and its High Street has a Georgian bridge that is steep enough to keep out most motor traffic (86). Because The Lodge is described as so aesthetically pleasing, the Harveys' planned depredations in the name of a government office are even more horrifying, making it easy to identify them, simply doing the best for their employer, as the villains of the piece, symbolizing as they do the "Brave New World" despoiling the beauties of the past (94-99).

By contrast, The Cedars is a much more modest, but still delightful brick house with two double storey bows, an efficient kitchen yard, and a stable with a charming antique clock (233). It is, then, quite aesthetically satisfying when the Harveys are bested in the first case by Lady Cora's appeal to Sir Cecil Waring and in the second by Maria Lufton's appeal to Oliver, and in each case, the architectural beauty is saved (100). The Cedars will be especially delightful in the future, as Oliver Marling's taste is "good and intelligent" (319). Another house that is much admired is that of Mr. Macpherson on the Rushwater estate, a perfect little Regency stucco house with delightful ornament, which becomes the home of Emmy Graham and Tom Grantly. The Rushwater valley, too, is lyrically described (295).

There are the usual aesthetically pleasing but vaguely generic descriptions of babies, in this case of Heather's son (21) and Lucy's daughter (35). But much as they are adored, Thirkell avers that children at a distance are more appealing and has the Grantlys, in a warm, rose-scented dusk, admit to each other "how nice it is when the [grown] children aren't here" (29). Other personal descriptions are more detailed, and the reader learns that Sir Cecil Waring is tall and thin with blue eyes (67), that Marigold the parlormaid has dirty hands, colored nails, and lank blond hair (80), that Lord Lufton has a "rather vague shambling appearance" (112) and a "rather spotty face" (113). Aesthetics are more particular in other descriptions. Lady Cora has beautiful bones and lovely dark eyes (126, 131), along with fine legs and a "sleek dark head" (92). Isabel Dale is "unusually beautiful" with her blond hair and blue eyes (93), as is Sylvia Leslie (125). Lord Lufton is stunned by Clarissa

Graham's beauty (124), and both Lady Cora and Leslie Winter admire Grace Grantly (250).

Thirkell continues to reference events of previous books, as characters nostalgically remember Heather Adams' fall through the ice (55, 58, 75), the Hosier's Girls' Foundation School awards day (59), the story of Sid Thatcher's success with Palafax Borealis (13), the awfulness of Dr. Morgan (59), Eric Swan's and Philip Winter's earlier days at Southbridge School (79, 249), Emmy Graham's childhood fall into a pond (174) and other such events. These reminiscences serve to remind the long-time reader of plot points and to give her a sense of being an insider in sharing this knowledge, but as many critics have pointed out, this rehashing becomes more and more frequent, even to the point of tediousness, as certain events are recalled multiple times even within the same book, as with the Heather Adams accident cited above.

Another element that is increasingly given attention is the weather. While not really an aesthetic concern, the untrustworthiness of the weather, usually in the guise of a cold, rainy summer, is commented upon with great frequency by both the author and her characters (119, 159). Because lovely summer days are much oftener and very lovingly described in the pre-war books, it would seem that Thirkell is having nature reflect the human condition, as the weather is so much worse in the post-war books. Here, too, as in previous post-war novels, she humorously links the bad weather to the Labour government (66).

CHAPTER V: POST WAR 1952-1961

In the later post war years, bouyed by her success in the United States, Angela Thirkell produced one a year, and traveled to the US to be greeted with enthusiasm by her US audience. Although she considered them formulaic, they introduce new characters and update her contented readers on old ones. This final set is comprised of *Happy Return, Jutland Cottage, What Did It Mean?, Enter Sir Robert, Never Too Late, A Double Affair, Close Quarters, Love at all Ages,* and her final book, *Three Score and Ten.*

Happy Return (1952)

The title of *Happy Return* is popularly supposed to refer to the return to power of the Conservative government in 1951, as well as to the return of the Bishop from a cruise to Madeira. It also serves as an indication of a return to many of the same characters as the previous book, notable Eric Swan and the Lufton family.

The beauty of the English landscape is the first aesthetic concern (9), and interestingly enough, the second is the improvement in the appearance of Marigold, the parlormaid at Beliers Priory, who is much less made up and has gained control of her hair, previously coiffed to emulate one of her movie heroines (11). Sir Cecil Waring remembers his first view of the stunning Lady Cora Palliser (23), and quite a lot is made of both Rose Fairweather's beauty and, by contrast, of her incredibly messy and revolting bedroom (31). Other personal descriptions are built around the Christmas ball at The Nabob, including Lady Graham's rose-coloured lace and Edith's elegant white chiffon dress (166) and other "delightful, descriptive passages, of the people, the food, and the setting" (Fritzer 107). A more effusive homage than usual is made to the memory of Lady Emily Leslie (197).

Another personal description relates to the impressiveness of both Lord Lufton and Grace Grantly when they are dressed in the baron's robes. Although Oliver and Clarissa play at dressing up, it is on the dignity of Lord Lufton, and even more on that and the beauty of Grace, that Thirkell concentrates. And it is seeing Grace in such a state that enthralls Eric Swan and convinces Lord Lufton he has found the woman to wear his mother's robes (220-221, 275).

Architecture and house furnishings come in for comment, as the Vicarage and church at St. Ewold's are described positively in some detail, with particular attention to the beauty of the upstairs view, but with the conclusion that "neither of [the Millers] had any particular taste" (40-41). Conversely, the description of the church hall at Pomfret Madrigal is humorously derisory (121), as is the description of Palafox Borealis (199-200), but the description of Harefield House is of perfectly proportioned beauty (150), as is that of the Old Bank House (200). Mrs. Joram praises her own house in the Close, just as Thirkell does in more detail (295)

Thirkell comments thankfully on the fact that the big national chain stores have so far stayed out of Harefield, finding it not practical "to invade so small a territory" (152). The ballroom at The Nabob, built by the Nabob, also comes in for much admiration of its fine architectural features (158, 184).

In *Happy Return*, Lady Lufton remarks that Mr. McFadyen has had the Canaletto cleaned (34), with no reference to its subject or merit, although to the reader this act on his part seems both presumptuous and dangerous—what if it had been damaged? A George Richmond drawing owned by Lady Lufton is described as having the highlight upon the tip of the nose which is almost a signature of that delightful artist (279).

Another beautiful luxury item is the "very cold" diamond spray of jewels Mrs. Belton shows Swan and Charles, as the latter thinks of Clarissa Graham (161-62). Similarly, Lady Lufton shows Grace Grantly a set of emerald jewelry in antique gold, an odd piece of which is used for her engagement ring (278). Thirkell doesn't give much attention to jewelry in the earlier books, as there are only passing mentions of symbolic jewels. There is a diamond and ruby spray Sam Adams gives Anne Fielding for her marriage in *Love Among the Ruins*, and, of course, the diamond ring old Miss Brandon gives to Mrs. Brandon in *The Brandons*. In *The Headmistress*, Christopher Hornby and Elsa Belton have a brief quarrel about some of his family jewelry, and she wears an antique engagement ring. The jewelry that is given the most attention is the ring with which Philip Winter and Rose Fairweather are engaged: its discard, recovery and reuse are threaded through several books and referenced many times more. Thirkell here and in several future books mentions with approval various jewels, seemingly as elements of tangibles to hold onto from the traditional past.

Nostalgia appears as Thirkell gives yet another peroration about those who fought in World War II, noting that "delayed war-shock is another of the gifts of modern civilization," and lamenting that in the area of warfare, science seems to harm faster than it seems to heal (105). She also has many reminiscences of events of past books, including Leslie Waring's unorthodox engagement (106), former days at Southbridge School (143), and dancing at Stories (246).

Jutland Cottage (1953)

Jutland Cottage is a real Cinderella story, as plump, awkward Margot Phelps is brought out of her shell and given a makeover by Rose Fairweather and friends, to earn three proposals by the end of the book. More than in other books, there is great aesthetic attention to clothes and grooming (131, 154, 171, 185,187, 205, 215 ,218, 221, 229, 269, 274), as Margot becomes more attractive with encouragement. The critics were not kind to this book: one called Margot Phelps a "damp sponge" (Walbridge 2323) and another called her a "middle-aged wad of human blotting paper" (*The New Yorker* 159). It is a favorite of many readers, however, perhaps because they like a bit of fashion, even if it is not Madame Koska. Thirkell notes here as she often does elsewhere that most women, far from being jealous, appreciate beauty in other women (35, 166).

Thirkell's sense of humor shows as she mixes regretful remarks by various characters about Margot's unfortunate appearance in trousers, with a later hilarious, unconsciously ironic, dissertation by Miss Hampton about not wearing trousers because her old father would not approve since "He liked a woman to be a woman" (53). Clearly, for some the economic situation is looking up, and the humor about it continues, as Hampton and Bent complain about the high cost of everything, then announce they have been skiing in Mixo-Lydia and are laying up a store of drinks (53). They follow up with the announcement that "Times are hard," so they are buying a new car, too (54).

There is, however, a level of anxiety about money that is much more real than in other books, i. e. the Phelps family is much closer to the margin and easier with which to identify, than are the Pomfrets or the Pallisers, poor rich folk. The last character who was truly penurious was Ella Morris, the poverty-stricken companion in *The Brandons*. On the part of various characters, there is a real bafflement here that there is really nothing Margot can do for money, a result of not having ever been self-supporting. There is also a strong reliance on the government to do something more for the admiral and for his wife, and a dismay that there is no pension for his daughter (110, 115-118, 228).

Tubby Fewling deplores the fact that the government requires widows to work if they are able, which rule one would think would be welcome to conservatives concerned about too many benefits being given to the populace. But Thirkell in this book seems to have absorbed some of the socialist feeling of the Labour government years about society providing a safety net. But for her, a convenient marriage is the answer to both Ella Morris's and Margot Phelps' dilemma, as it will be later to Dorothea Merriman's problem of being unwanted when she is no longer needed to help the Leslie family, although her situation is not so financially desperate. Jennifer Nesbitt suggests that "Perhaps because of her unconventional early life [two divorces and the stigma they carried], her novels are conservative reiterations of marriage plot after marriage plot" (16). Additionally, Rachel Mather points out that for Thirkell, "Marriage as happy ending . . . reflects society's position" (61).

From a rehashing of the history of the Leslie family (8), Thirkell brings the reader up on the fact that the John Leslies have bought and are living in the very pleasant Old Rectory at Greshamsbury, though neither of them "had much of what is called taste" (9). This information is followed by a very funny description of upscale "improvements" to some of the cottages in the village (21). The church itself "had not suffered too much from zealous hands," except for the "unfortunate" Memorial Window (22-23). This church is much more attractive than the one at Southbridge School, which perhaps not surprisingly is a Victorian excrescence, because it was designed by the architect of Pomfret Towers, another monument to bad taste (45), as is Beliers Priory, "the most hideous mansion in Barsetshire" (186).

This description is in contrast to the Crofts' drawing room, which, despite being of awkward proportions, is tastefully decorated with good curtains and family portraits by Raeburn and Lawrence (45). Finally, Harefield House, now the Winters' school, is described again, as is the lovely view across the downs (262).

Tubby Fewling relates a heartfelt and nostalgic historically true anecdote about an air raid during the war and the noble behavior of George VI, much appreciated by the people (26), which leads into a discussion about whether the monarchy has a future (29).

Nature is paid tribute with a description of the view from a high road, across downs, the Woolram valley, and the water meadows, with a notation that the land and villages were very little changed (41). Similarly, Lady Cora and Margot look out admiringly at the view over the downs from Mr. Wickham's delightfully described summerhouse (159).

A very funny personal description is that of Mrs. Feeder, a very traditional-looking, thin little old lady who smokes, who is a heavy drinker, and who can match wits with any guest of Wiple Terrace (42, 57). The usual admiration of Rose Fairweather is cited (83, 89, 118, 244-45).

Nostalgia is served by a delightful recollection of Mrs. Villars about Captain Holden at Northbridge Rectory during the war, from the book of that name (88). Another more lengthy recollection is of the Christmas party for the evacuee children that was a central incident in *Cheerfulness Breaks In* (99), and Mary Leslie recalls her engagement from *Wild Strawberries* (109). Rose Fairweather tells her luncheon companions about the summer she was engaged to Philip Winter (208).

As for art, David Leslie references a ubiquitous traditional banal print "Bolton Abbey in the Olden Times" (12), and Kate Carter remarks upon the "awful coloured cards of beauty spots" that the artist Mr. Scatcherd has in the past deplored for taking away his livelihood. Swan tells Justinia Lufton that she looks like the beauty in the Richmond portrait, the same one referenced in the previous book, with remarks here about the highlighted nose that was common in early portraits (266-67).

Finally, music has more of a place in this book than in others. Lady Lufton plays the piano beautifully, and Mr. Macfadyen sings, as Eric Swan is moved by the beauty of the music (241). Later, he also nostalgically remembers Mr. Macfadyen's singing of a sad and evocative song the previous year at Lady Lufton's, which leads to a discussion of German music with that gentleman (264).

What Did It Mean? (1954)

What Did It Mean? has as its main theme the coronation of Queen Elizabeth II. As Thirkell highlights the idiosyncrasies and foibles of villagers working toward a common goal, the book has much the flavor of *Northbridge Rectory*, set in the same village during the war, in which the villagers worked similarly toward a common effort. Consequently, it is one of the strongest of the later books, despite its being loaded with nostalgia. It is also a favorite because, after emphasis on several new characters in the previous books, there is the comfort of familiar characters such as Lydia Merton, the Pomfrets, and Jessica Dean and Aubrey Clover, who have kindly agreed to put on a playlet for the local celebration. Aubrey, that experienced player, has an amusing description of the expected hazards of the makeshift stage (199).

What Did It Mean plunges right into nostalgia at the beginning with a reminiscence by Lady Cora about the day Sir Cecil Waring (in *The Duke's Daughter*) had to be rushed to the hospital (8), and shortly Lydia Merton is happily remembering the Pomfret Madrigal Fete (from *The Brandons*) when she was a teenager (17), and ruefully remembering how much better the railways were before the war (21). Mr. Villars recalls with Mr. Holden an air

iring the war (28), while Miss Pemberton
; Mrs. Paxon as a practice hysteria case
the latter from *Northbridge Rectory*)
(....) The high-energy Mrs. Paxon must have
been quite histrionic, because Mrs. Turner later
also remembers her performance (162).

What Did It Mean? also contains a look
back at Pomfret Towers in its glory days of
house parties before the war (33, 45),
including Lord Pomfret laughing at himself as a
young man dealing with the servants (36-7).
Lydia Merton continues with the usual
judgment, "I've seen the outside and it's pretty
ghastly" (44). Lydia also wistfully recalls her
boldness during earlier days for her and Colin
(58-59), the long-ago picnic on Parsley Island
(135), and, more unhappily, the summer of
Noel's flirtation with Mrs. Arbuthnot (101).
Lydia later falls into a frenzy of remembering
multiple incidents in the past (136-37, 144-
147), and there is a recounting of the
Pomfrets' engagement (227).

There is also a remembrance of the
Bishop's perilous cruise (241), and, for the first
time, the Bishop makes a slightly extended
appearance, during which he seems hen-
pecked but human (239-249). Even the
Bishopess thaws and discusses needlework
with the other ladies (247). That dinner party
at which they appear is also the venue for a lot
of recollection of the past, including Noel

Merton's and Mrs. Brandon's early flirtation and the Harveys' past in Barsetshire (250-55).

On a personally descriptive level, Aubrey Clover thinks of Lydia, who has never really been physically described beyond her early robustness, sunburn, and torn dress in *Summer Half*. He muses that she is "Handsome, good-looking, perhaps noble, full of character, a face with shadows and reticences, a face in which enduring love might make its mark: but pretty, no" (82). Except for the brown eyes Lydia remarks on here (101), the reader still is left not knowing what she looks like, a common problem with many of Thirkell's main characters, since her descriptions of them tend to be evocative rather than concrete, a wise withholding that allows the reader to fill in with his or her imagination, just as the reader fills in with imagination the feelings of Lydia and Lord Pomfret in several passages of restrained but significant glances (121), reinforced by Eleanor Keith's remarks and queries about why Lydia is looking so well (130). The very attractive Mrs. Brandon, described so generically in previous books, here has "hair that wreathed itself into silver-grey tendrils" (208), a description used previously in other books of both Selena Hopkins and Mrs. Turner.

Jessica Dean is a main character here, her husband as amusing and talented as ever but deliberately allowing himself as usual to be overshadowed by his wife. Thirkell writes a very funny descriptive passage of Aubrey Clover "disguised" as a country character with pipe and shooting jacket, as he researches the speech of one of the rural locals, pointing up again Thirkell's frequent assertion in multiple books that Aubrey can blend in anywhere, taking on the persona of anyone he chooses (79-81). Jessica, with her confidence, her beauty, "an exquisite portrait like a Romney" and her speech affections of "my sweet" and "Too, too lovely to see you," brings to the reader's mind Clarissa Belton and Rose Birkett Fairweather, as well as Lady Cora (79).

Throughout, there is much description of Ludovic Foster and his amazing height, which turns out later to be six foot, two inches, so the modern reader wonders a bit. Thirkell, who always does uncertain young people so well, seems really very fond of Ludo, and there are sprinkled throughout many, many sympathetic remarks about him by the other characters (97-101).

There are the usual swipes about the hideousness of Pomfret Towers, but other architecture is not so significant in this book. For Pomfret Towers, there is a more extensive description than usual, in which the reader learns in additional gory detail just how awful the much-maligned architecture really is (190-92, 195, 218-19, 223, 225-26). It is odd that there are two complete and descriptive tours of the house very close together, one for the Mertons and one for the Adamses, and in the first one the chapel has ugly windows (195), but in the second one, it is very beautiful (226). Lucy Adams, visiting the house for the first time in years, remarks "Gosh! I remembered it was awful, but I'd forgotten it was as awful as that" (218). The enormous and ugly house is a symbol of oppression for the Pomfrets, and throughout this book, it is made apparent how precarious their financial position is, not in terms of ordinary folk, but in relation to their class. Sam Adams, then, becomes the rescuer of yet another upper-class Barsetshire family (after helping out Mr. Belton and Mr. Marling, and saving the Old Bank House) and he will ride to the rescue yet again by leasing The Towers of the Duke of Towers in *Love at All Ages*.

A much less significant architectural description is that of Punshions, Miss Pemberton's cottage that was, in typically unsentimental Thirkell fashion, "as uncomfortable as only an old stone cottage can be," with its cold stone floor, its drafty fireplace, its low beams, its uneven floors (149). The bucolic countryside is represented by a description of the Bunces' thatched cottage, "looking incredibly [artist George] Morlandesque" along with its pipe-smoking inhabitant, who exchanges Anglo-Saxon insults with his daughters (126).

Punshions gets attention here because this is the book in which, after many recollections of Northbridge during the war (275, 278), including of their nascent romance, Mrs. Turner finally agrees to marry Mr. Downing (290-291), and Miss Pemberton dies, giving her blessing beforehand (318). Mrs. Turner still has silver hair curling in tendrils (277, 298).

Perhaps because *What Did It Mean?* is so full of nostalgia, the weather cooperates. In echoes of childhood, Colin Keith is able to swim at his childhood home and to take the children out in the punt, since the weather "was getting really hot," (131), "was still warm and fine" (134), and "the heat was quite delightful" (137). When the Mertons visit Pomfret Towers, "The weather--by a serious oversight on its own part—was again fairly warm," and there are rare kind words for the outside of the building and its Italian gardens (187, 220).

Finally, *What Did It Mean?* ends with an extended and witty description of the pageant so earnestly performed after so much effort (305-317). The music, the costumes, the audience are all wryly but fondly dissected and humor reigns supreme.

Enter Sir Robert (1955)

Enter Sir Robert is supposed to be the Thirkell in which, more than most, nothing happens, since there are no engagements. This book and the next two, *Never Too Late* and *A Double Affair*, read like segments of the same book. Cynthia Snowden points out story arcs across various books (xiii-xiv), but she does not note that these particular three are intimately entwined. It is not only Edith Graham who is the focus of these, but, to a lesser extent, George Halliday and John-Arthur Crosse, who come more to the fore in *A Double Affair*, leaving Edith still floundering. "Edith is too slight and uninteresting a figure . . . Edith . . . in her ambiguousness is more suited to supporting character status" (Fritzer 8).

The two men are sympathetic characters, scarred as they are by the war, which has left them feeling nostalgic and old for their ages, and their friendship is delicately shown. Like Tom Grantly, both are restless but settling into civilian life, and John-Arthur in particular seems anxious to get his life in established order, as will be seen from the haste in which he later proposes in *A Double Affair* to an eminently suitable girl whom he barely knows.

99

Again, perhaps because not as much ppens in *Enter Sir Robert*, for most areas, iere are fewer descriptions and aesthetic passages. The book opens with several pages of charming description of Hatch End, as the author notes in the form of a reminder that not only the Hallidays live there, but so do the Grahams [in nearby Little Misfit] (3-7).

The vicar Mr. Choyce, who will play a much larger role in the next book, is a pertinent character here, with multiple iterations of his desire for a wife. His monkey puzzle tree is mentioned often with opprobrium (14, 52) and Thirkell with wry humor notes that "His study . . . was so exactly like a study that words are not needed. If we say that there were coloured Arundel prints on the wall . . . and a hockey stick over the mantelpiece, we shall have said quite enough" (14). Thirkell's great way with evocative description is shown here, as is her use of a kind of shorthand to prompt the reader's imagination. Although Thirkell sometimes indulges herself in deliberately long-winded descriptions of minutiae, she often does the opposite, as she does above and here: "There is no need for us to describe the Morning Service in a village church, for it is part of our life" (107).

There is the usual talk of the weather, but this book has a tremendous amount of bad weather ("nasty chill grey day[s]") (76), more than in previous books, perhaps as an

100

indication of the unsettledness of life in general. It includes a very funny passage averring that because of foreigners, "the Atom Bomb and Crashing the Sound Barrier (or whatever it is) and the General March of Progress, the weather is going to be worse and worse for ever and ever" (71). It is this kind of curmudgeonly material that Thirkell's acolytes find so amusing and that many others find so annoying. H. W. Chapman makes a good analysis about appreciating the humor of her descriptions and not taking them too literally:

> I find it difficult to understand the point of view of those whom this author has irritated, as I recall it, to madness. The Labour Government seems to worry her a bit, and every now and then there is a nostalgic reference to Mr. Churchill and his days of power (Ah! Those were the times, when we were all killing one another), while foreigners, intellectuals and working-class folk are treated as figures of fun. But what of it? (722).

On a personally descriptive level Thirkell gives a very complete look at the costume of Mr. Scatcherd, the untalented but ubiquitous and stereotypical artist (20-21). His awful little purple-brick house, which has been described in detail in earlier books, is revisited and seems not to have improved, nor has his famous drawing of the cathedral, appearing to most viewers as large bulrushes (33-37).

Another personal description, a much more emotional one, is that of Mr. Halliday, whose wife "noticed with a pang how old his hands looked . . . a little tremulous," another indication that he is clearly not well (134). Emotion is described more often in *Enter Sir Robert* than in most of the other Barsetshire books, and another instance is Thirkell's "divagation" about the way melancholy popular music can appeal to one's "lowest and most penny-novelette feelings," causing one to be overcome with weeping (150).

George Halliday and his father look out over the beautiful land: "Barsetshire lay at his feet like a map, as lovely a county as any," with fulsome description of its natural beauties (72). Nature is further represented by the flowers put in the church for a memorial service for Lady Emily, dead some years, and the class divide in taste is represented by the lilies and delphiniums Mr. Choyce and Lady Graham bring, as differentiated from the "cottage garden bequests, very compact, their stalks tightly bound with coloured plastic tape . . . strange lifeless products of the Brave New World" (40-41).

Architecture is served with a description of the Old Manor House at Hatch End: the hall is "elegantly proportioned" with a "gentlemanly staircase" and charming reception rooms with nice views (120). The drawing room, with its beautiful floor, bow window, and Chinese wallpaper, leaves Mrs. Halliday breathless (125), while the rest of the house is just as lovely (155-58), as is the grotto at Cross Hall (234), itself a charming, comfortable period house with good windows and old brick (221). The beauty of the Saloon at Holdings, with its long windows, faded brocade curtains, and marble fireplace is lovingly described (192), The Close, too, is as beautiful as ever (98), as is the arched bridge at Starveacres Hatches with its perfectly proportioned railings (239).

It is while walking in the Close with George Halliday that Edith Graham remembers the incident of the bell in the Bishop's fishpond (101). Similarly, Lady Graham is nostalgic for her brothers' youth, although her memories of them stomping beetles is not very romantic (111). Peters the butler and Miss Merriman remember the old days at Pomfret Towers (230), and there is a lot of nostalgic chat tracing back the various families (232). Lady Graham and Mrs. Morland have an orgy of remembering lovely Lady Emily and tedious Mr. Holt (267-68).

As in the later *A Double Affair*, there are some nicely delicate descriptions about young and old rubbing up against each other. Here, Mrs. Halliday is an eminently reasonable woman who thinks of George, as he takes the lead in running the farm, "Prince Hal is trying on the crown," and she wonders "why the young were . . . such a mixture of callousness and intense sensitiveness" (113).   Similar wondering takes place on George's part when he is "uncomfortable" at his father's emotional speech, "for when our elders make an appeal, even unconsciously, to our emotions, we are apt to . . . feel outraged" (70).

Never Too Late (1956)

Never Too Late continues the saga of Edith Graham trying to find herself. As usual, Thirkell does restless young people very well. There are, however, far too many references to Clarissa's tip tilted fingers (169), and many, many comparisons of Edith to her sisters, Clarissa and Emmy Graham. Thirkell seems to be simply marking time in this book as far as the development of Edith Graham is concerned.   Interestingly, Mr. Richard Carter, Lord Crosse's son-in-law, thinks of Edith that she "would be an extremely useful person in the county, though of course she was bound to marry and throw it all away," a rather surprisingly negative statement for Thirkell to make about marriage, and one that will, of course, come true by *Love at All Ages* (200-01).

In a departure from their usual presentation, the Pomfrets look rather opportunistic when Miss Merriman apparently breaks down from exhaustion working for them.   One wonders what work they are all doing that is so exhausting, as they are not exactly coal miners. Further, Miss Merriman is not that old: she was older than Gillie Foster in 1938's *Pomfret Towers*, so she could have been as young as perhaps twenty-five or as old as perhaps forty, which twenty years later would have made her as young as forty-five or as old as sixty, or somewhere between, hardly in her dotage.

The Pomfrets quickly hire Miss Updike permanently (301) when Merry has simply gone to the Grahams' for a visit to rest "for a week or so" (299). It is clear that they do not intend to take her back and she seems to know that (178). Indeed, Mr. Choyce seems almost to have made one of Mr. Wickham's pity proposals, as he doesn't ask Miss Merriman to marry him (312) until, after making a speech about her duty and love for the Leslies and Pomfrets (284), she announces that "Service is no inheritance . . . I have enough money to live on, simply. But the life I have led for so long must soon come to an end and I must start again," as she dissolves in tears (311). And the Pomfrets and the Grahams are almost indecently enthusiastic about the wedding, which will solve the problem for them of an unwanted dependent. One cannot help thinking that that "most unpleasant Miss Harvey" (6), despite her many faults, made a better decision with her career, which will not leave her dependent in her old age.

This book opens with a return to High Rising and a sumptuous tea at Mrs. Morland's house there (15). Much is made of the improvement in Lord Mellings (16-17), although his development is almost as slow as is that of Edith, with many repetitious remarks (164) but not a lot of progress. Similarly, both John-Arthur Crosse and George Halliday are still trying to readjust to civilian life (22, 156).

There is a rather inexplicable interlude early in the book at a party at Southbridge School, in which Manners, a young man who had been an evacuee there during the war and who is now a professor, drops in and asks to speak with Rose Fairweather (52-53). Although his appearance is the occasion for much reminiscing, it develops that Rose has never met him because she was in South America with her husband, although she recalls her sister Geraldine's description of him (53-54). After some chitchat, he offers to dedicate his next book to Rose and invites her and her husband to tea, before taking his leave (55). Never is it explained why he feels so kindly toward her. One might almost wonder if Thirkell began the anecdote, did a little fact-checking, and didn't want to lose what she had written, so just kept going with a bit of adaptation.

On the aesthetic side, Thirkell says of Mrs. Morland (and of herself?) that she is "on the whole indifferent to her surroundings," and that the furniture was comfortable but not of any particular note (26), interesting information from an author who is so often concerned with beauty in architecture and, to a lesser extent, in furnishings. There is more from Mrs. Morland, who, clearly speaking as Thirkell, does a very funny extemporation on her books, including one written under a pseudonym, from Mrs. Morland's description, a combined obvious reference to *Trooper to the Southern Cross* and *The Fortunes of Harriet* (82-85, 155). She follows up with Mrs. Morland musing about fan mail and the problems of authorship (194-95, 201). Near the end of the book, Mrs. Morland also leads a conversation with Lord Crosse about using people's names in books, people who take offence and think the names are theirs, and possible lawsuits resulting from such use (286-87). This passage is particularly amusing, since Strickland relates that the real Lord Cross had made such a fuss about his name being used in the previous *Enter Sir Robert* that here in *Never Too Late* the spelling of the character's name has been changed to "Crosse" (Strickland 164).

Mrs. Morland may not care much about her surroundings, but Mrs. Thirkell does, because the Old Manor House at Hatch End, introduced in *Enter Sir Robert*, is lovingly described in all its restored glory. Lady Graham sees that "both understanding and money were being given to the house," and she appreciates its paint, polish, new curtains, and lovely old oriental rug (117).

There are also descriptions of the rustic views over the downs from the big, comfortable rooms (119, 127).

Punshions, the stone cottage at Northbridge where the three nurses live, has become more comfortable but has had its spare authenticity ruined with paint, carpets, and a gas fire (213). "[T]heir friends said it was too cosy for words [not a word viewed by the upper classes as a compliment to taste]. As indeed it was, but better be cosy than cold any time" (213).

Another architectural description, one typical of Thirkell in its elegiac quality of nostalgia and beauty, both man-made and natural, is of the village of Hatch End:

> with its mixture of Saxon wattle and daub with fine stone and brick houses, and the ground rising away from the river and undulating to the noble line of the downs where corn was ripe and sheep bells were tinkling and the mellow afternoon sun was over all. (279-80)

In regards to nostalgia, Edith Graham and Mrs. Morland discuss the war, with further explanation of why one might miss it, as Edith references "the way people did things for other people in the war and nearly everyone got so nice . . ." (28). Similarly, Eileen of the Red Lion says "Me and matron we often say we wish the war was on again. Those were the days" (49). Because Southbridge and Southbridge School are early settings, there is also a lot of explication about various characters and their relationships (31), and about past events in Barsetshire (39-59), including a visit by the revolting Mr. Holt (157) who was also remembered for no particular reason in *Enter Sir Robert*.

Tony Morland appears and kisses his "Mamma's" hand (41), in a manner reminiscent of that of Francis Brandon and his teasing relationship with his mother in *The Brandons*. Peters, the butler, reminisces with Edith about Julian Rivers' long-ago visit to Pomfret Towers (88), and Edith reminisces with Mrs. Morland about a past Bring and Buy sale (99). There is also a lot of laughter and talk about old photos, with much nostalgia for the times they represented (161-62). One wonders whether perhaps such discussion is in aid of the author's memory as much as it is to aid the reader's.

Personal description is most pleasing as applied to Rose Fairweather, "an entrancing apparition" in her beautiful clothes and shoes (51). Rose's description is in contrast to the description of Miss Bent in her bedraggled bohemian outfit "calculated to show off even the slimmest and most elegant figure [not Miss Bent's] to great disadvantage" (58). Miss Hampton is in her usual uniform of a "gentlemanly black suit with a white silk shirt and a stock, black silk stockings, and very neat black shoes with silver buckles" (58). Mrs. Feeder, whose presentation is generally positive, is quite amusing with her "glittering eyes, bony figure, and claw-like hands covered with rings" (59). By contrast Mrs. Richard Carter's babies are described with the usual enthusiasm for babies (181, 203, 206). With her softness and her excellent domestic sense, Mrs. Everard Carter (Kate) in this book appears to be a younger incarnation of Lady Agnes Graham (196-99).

The weather is nasty as ever (67), and throughout the book there are constant references to people being cold (151), surely a reflection of Thirkell's own circumstances as she wrote it. Margot Strickland says of Thirkell in this period that "Habits of frugality . . . combined with the dreariness of living alone, had made her undernourished" (Strickland 166). Perhaps that explains one of the most sensual, enchanting descriptions to appear in any of the books, that of the Sunday roast beef lunch at Holdings, that goes on for several pages with special attention to the quality of the beef, the gravy, the potatoes, the sauce, the French beans, and the salad (153), as well as the raspberry fool and cream, the spongecake, and the coffee (159). One wonders when Thirkell had had her last decent meal when she wrote this, since by the time of Mrs. Carter's later dinner party, there is much description of the party (193) but virtually none of the "good dinner" and "excellent wine" (196).

By siding with the untalented, posturing artist Mr. Scatcherd (220-25) against the son of Lord Aberfordbury (formerly Sir Ogilvy Hibberd) and his post card enterprise, the assembled company gets yet another opportunity to resist the modernization of Barsetshire (202). Another art remark involves Senor Garcia of Argentina, who turns up to buy "any pictures of chocolate-box English beauty" (285).

Babies also are mentioned favorably again (203-04, 206), as is the Junoesque Sylvia Leslie with her "shining golden hair" (235). She comes to visit as her father is ill, and there is a touching vignette in close detail of Hubback, the Halliday's maid, fixing up Nurse Heath's room, sinking any dissention as everyone worries about Mr. Halliday (232-33).

Thirkell is excellent at beautifully delineating confusion in some of her old people. She does it very well in several previous books for Lady Emily Leslie, she does it very well in later books for Admiral and Mrs. Phelps, and she does it very well throughout *Never Too Late* for Mr. Halliday, as he alternates increasingly disconnected remarks with less frequent lucidity. Thirkell says at one point that after a relevant remark, "he relapsed into his usual state of withdrawal into some far place where his wife could not reach him," a description familiar to those with experience in the confusion of some elders (237). Mr. Halliday, however, is not completely out of touch, and despite his son's and his wife's misgivings (241-42), has managed to insure the estate against death duties, allowing George to carry on farming it. Other elders, like Sir Edmund Pridham or old Lord Stoke, never seem to lose their bite and efficiency.

Thirkell is also sensitive to the strains of a death watch, perhaps after having gone through such with relatives, and has a very delicate description of Mrs. Halliday waiting for the end while her husband is dying (256-57), and of the country reaction to that event (258-63). Thirkell is never mawkish, but examines internal feelings with empathy, humor, and resignation.

A Double Affair (1957)

A Double Affair is interesting in its title because the two romances to which that title refers are not even introduced until about halfway through the book. The Crawley granddaughters, Jane and Grace, are mentioned by name but do not make an appearance until late, so the courtship is very rushed, to say the least. Although George Halliday and Jane Crawley remember each other as children and see each other several times before becoming affianced, John-Arthur Crosse doesn't even meet Jane until page 221, and she apparently introduces him to Grace Crawley before the dinner at the White Hart, after which both couples become engaged, because even John–Arthur is abashed at the haste of their courtship, saying "I have only met Grace a few times but I think I fell in love the first time only I didn't know it" (245). In a personal description reminiscent of that of Isabel Dale, each of the girls, one fair and one dark, has "a face of that Victorian oval which one now so rarely sees" (194) and they are both apparently very good-looking (205, 267). Both have jobs and so are examples of Thirkell's adaptation to the modern post-war climate for young women, although each of them is, like the young men, happy to marry in haste.

Thirkell seems to have painted herself into a corner with Edith Graham, and does not seem able to move her forward or to think of anything for her to do. Edith doesn't change from book to book, so reading these three in rapid sequence is very repetitious. In this last book featuring her, there is a foreshadowing that she will marry, and Thirkell, reports the engagement in a very understated way in *Close Quarters*, so understated in fact that Jill Levin says "We see almost nothing of her courtship—a curiously significant omission for a novelist who wrote about almost nothing else" (131). It would seem that Thirkell suddenly just got tired of Edith and wanted to get rid of her in the quickest and easiest way, and she will be next presented in *Love at All Ages* as a contented young mother whose baby is about to be christened.

There is a quite shocking statement here in *A Double Affair* in relation to Miss Merriman's wedding, with which the book begins. After many, many comments over many, many books about Miss Merriman's devotion to the upper class, "the class she chose to serve all her life," Thirkell writes that Lord and Lady Pomfret "had not been able to get away from their duties in time to go to the church and now only had time to put in an appearance for the pleasure of congratulating their faithful friend and helper" (80). A harsh critic might be tempted to note that it is difficult to imagine what duties could have prevented them from attending the wedding of someone they cared about, the same someone they replaced at the first sign of neediness after her years of working and caring for them.

From another, more kindly and understanding point of view, Susan Scanlon writes:

I don't think Thirkell meant [the Pomfrets] to be so callous about Merry. I think it was a symptom of Angela Thirkell's general falling-apartness in the final books. There is nothing in the early or middle books that would make one think that they had anything but affection and gratitude to Merry, and they would certainly know their duty to her, if nothing else. (private letter)

Following Scanlon's lead, one might, then, think of the Pomfrets' missing Merry's wedding as another instance of Thirkell's again relating their excessive devotion to duty. The Graham family rescues Miss Merriman by having her to stay and by sponsoring her wedding. Lady Graham provides the gown and reception and plans the whole wedding (6-10), Clarissa arranges the flowers (75) and the elusive Sir Robert walks Miss Merriman down the aisle (77). David Leslie, for once seeming sincere, has a kind and nostalgic discussion with Miss Merriman about her happiness, after which they both mourn Lady Emily yet again (55). Mrs. Morland, though a more casual friend, kindly offers her house at High Rising for the honeymoon (11), a good thing, since, despite some very nice wedding gifts from the Pomfrets, the villa at Cap Ferrat, which will be offered to Lady Gwendolen Harcourt and Mr. Caleb Oriel in *Love at All Ages* (144), does not seem to be on offer for Miss Merriman and Mr Choyce.

There are charming descriptions of the arrangements for displaying the wedding gifts (*A Double Affair* 6-7), the wedding dress (9-10), the delightfully old-fashioned clothing of Mr. Gresham the best man (75), the garish gift of a nightgown case from Nurse (21), the beautiful gift of old Lady Pomfret's brooch from the current Lord and Lady Pomfret (22-23), and the miserly gift from the Bishop and his wife (60-61). Luxurious presents, brought by Edith from America, are also lovingly described (68), as are the pretty dresses she and Rose Fairweather each brings back with her (146-47, 159-160).

On a personal level, Mr. Scatcherd makes an appearance in his usual stereotypical painting costume (39), and Sylvia Leslie is still golden (102). The attendees at a dinner party try to decide what a "Landed Proprietor" should look like, with everyone thinking of the Caldecott illustrations for Washington Irving's "Bracebridge Hall" (152). A funnier aesthetic element is provided by the dinner party at Glycerine Cottage, with its horrible faux-French decoration and food (166-78).

Thirkell makes a nice analysis of the aesthetic improvement in Pomfret Towers, hideous as it is, since its lease to Mr. Adams' group has brought new prosperity to the park (12-13), although the building has been unavoidably partitioned and changed to make it suitable for its new use (29). The chapel, however, has been preserved and is described in all its lapis lazuli and marble glory (30). Similarly, the beauty of the High Street of Northbridge, with its "lovely curve," "graceful Rennie bridge," raised Town Hall, and elegant old houses, is lauded (125). Hovis House is spoken of approvingly (132), as is its George

Richmond drawing with its trademark highlighted nose (126), which will act as a plot point to bring together Mrs. Dunsford and Mrs. Halliday (140).

Aesthetic and nostalgic appeal are provided by music, as Tubby Fewling "played himself into some of the music that makes one delightfully nostalgic" (161). Old music hall songs, songs from World War I, German songs, and waltzes are all part of his repertoire, and "the older men would have cried if they had not forgotten how," while the ladies were in "a kind of nostalgic dream" (161), like emotions evoked by Lady Cora's singing "Keep the Home Fires Burning" in *County Chronicle*. Early in the book, much of the nostalgia is provided by memories of Pomfret Towers before the war (23, 28), and Lady Graham remembers with David the summer of Martin's seventeenth birthday from *Wild Strawberries.*

Another thread of description is neither aesthetic nor nostalgic, but is both delicate and heartfelt, and that is the description of how irritating the widowed Mrs. Halliday is. Sylvia, having her mother to stay at Rushwater, finds her "almost as wearing as the drop of water on the stone" (105), and George dreads her return to Hatch End (105-108). Mrs. Halliday is even irritating to Edith, who shows her good manners by kindness to the older woman (120-122, 140). But in fairness, Thirkell notes that "what Mrs. Halliday thought no one had enquired . . . But the position of queen-mother is not easy" (114).

Thirkell also has Lady Graham referencing a poem about "how heavenly it would be if [Edith] were married and off [one's] hands (113), so it is not only the older generation that is annoying. Perhaps Thirkell's view is best summed up in her disquisition about the fact that the generations are better off not living together, especially if the older generation cannot give up control (105). Thirkell's father J. W. Mackail had died suddenly in 1945, and according to Margot Strickland, Thirkell's mother, Margaret Mackail, died in 1953 "after long years as a permanent invalid" (Strickland 159). It is perhaps this experience of caring for the widow that informs the treatment of Mrs. Halliday and even Mrs. Dunsford here, and later in *Close Quarters* the extensive treatment of the deaths of Margot Phelps Macfadyen's parents and her response.

Finally, *A Double Affair* also seems an applicable title in another way. Several events of the book are related twice, for no identifiable reason. Miss Merriman and Mr. Choyce seem to leave the church twice (78-70), and David Leslie is amazed at the idea of Lord Lufton and Edith, although he has earlier heard the suggestion (58). George Halliday is surprised to see Edith, even though he has been told by Mr. Panter that she is back (64), and Lady Graham suggests brightly that they talk about Merry's wedding (59), although they have just talked about it (50). Apparently, Margaret Bird pointed out to Thirkell many of the inconsistencies and repetitions that appeared in the first draft of the later *Love at All Ages* (Strickland 171), but they seem to have crept earlier into *A Double Affair*. Given that there are so many characters and relationships to juggle, Barbara Burrell says forgivingly, "It is no wonder that she occasionally lost track of what she had done" (vii).

Close Quarters (1958)

Apparently tired of Edith Graham, Thirkell mentions Edith's engagement to Lord William Harcourt early in *Close Quarters* (5, 207), then again turns her attention to Margot Phelps and Tubby Fewling. Donald Macfadyen's death, at a time when Thirkell was herself in not very good health (Strickland 169), is handled very delicately (63), as is Margot's sincere and grateful devotion to him (112-13, 120-21, 158). And the desire of older people to keep their independence is handled with great sympathy (65-66). But Margot's response to Donald's death, and to those of her parents, seems peripatetic, as Margot spends most of the book traveling around the county staying with friends and lackadaisically looking for a house, until Tubby rescues her with a proposal (281).

Margot is so reluctant about living with her parent(s) again that her widowed father is farmed out to Tubby Fewling while she makes a series of visits around the countryside. She very much loves and wishes to help her father, but flatly refuses to move too close for fear of being devoured as she was as a younger woman, and she is exhausted and dismayed by the whole problem. There is so much throughout the book about Margot's conflicted feelings that one cannot help wondering if writing it might have been a kind of catharsis for Thirkell, who had been through similar difficulties with her own parents [after years of illness, her mother died in 1953, the same year *Jutland Cottage* was published]. (Fritzer 74)

There are many, many recollections of Margot and the drudgery of her life before she married (77, 99-100, 104, 112, 116-17, 124, 182), and Mr. Wickham puts the matter quite plainly when he says if she lives near her parents again, she will be "eaten alive" (88). Even given that danger, it seems a bit hard on the confused old Admiral to be taken from his home immediately after his wife's death to stay with Tubby Fewling, because Margot doesn't want to stay with him. Perhaps Sister Chiffinch, there for a night or two, is not available longer term, although she agrees to stay on at Tubby's for a while (266). One can't quite make out why he couldn't be at home, at least for a while, given that he asks pitifully at Tubby's "Why am I here?" (265).

Marrying Tubby will mean moving to the Close of Barchester Cathedral, so Thirkell is given scope to describe again the loveliness of the area with its beautiful cathedral and charming old houses, which she does in great detail (274-75). The dean, in fact, lures Canon Fewling with the promise of the lovely Acacia House he will gain if he agrees to come to the Close (270-75).

Early on, Thirkell propounds her architectural opinions, at first quite different ones than usual. She notes that most of the old village houses are still there, but says they are not worth saving with their crumbling walls, holey thatch, and sooty water-catching chimneys, so that "it was cheaper and more sanitary to rebuild" (15). Just as the reader is catching her breath from such ideas coming from Thirkell, she gives a delightful, long passage about the hideousness and discomfort resulting from the remodeling of many New Town houses (16), so she is back in form. The Drill Hall for the Bring and Buy is a "horrid place" (18). A more pleasant place is Southbridge School, with its ugly "mid-Victorian Neo-Gothic chapel" and its welcoming friends (67). A journey to Northbridge evokes a charming description of the water meadows, the downs, and the "beautiful old stone bridge"

121

(98), as a journey to Harefield evokes a similarly charming description of that town and its High Street (118).

The Updike's house comes in for particular praise, with its beautiful staircase, well-proportioned hall, and cupola lit by natural light (119-20), as does the Beltons' Arcot House with its white paneling, fine furniture and paintings (158). Harefield House is lyrically described several times, and is so beautiful that Margot Macfadyen says "It's Perfect" (188), and there is an extended business of putting up the stored statues in the wings' alcoves (189-200). By contrast, Mr. Belton points out that "Omnium is a shocking monstrosity, so is Pomfret Towers—all the big houses. There are plenty of good small ones . . . . Barsetshire did best in the good red-brick period, with houses for the smaller landed gentry" (193).

The Parkinsons appear in *Close Quarters* and their background is explained yet again (12, 19-20), although the author seems almost envious of the delightful snug, new house she has given them (20) and there is rather too much about their new washing machine (30-31, 143). Thirkell delicately limns the Parkinsons as they attend their first dinner party in the Old Town (40-51), where it is discovered that Mrs. Parkinson has a delightful singing voice (53). One oddity is that Mr. Wickham attends that party and admires Mrs.

Parkinson's voice, but doesn't ever seem to have met the Parkinsons when Rose Fairweather much later in the book says the Parkinsons are coming to tea and Wickham asks who they are and doesn't seem to remember even with prodding (125).

There is continued nostalgia as Rose Fairweather remembers the Mixo-Lydian refugees during the war, and engages with them at the current Bring and Buy (23-25). Mr. Oriel and Mr. Belton have a fine time remembering their childhoods (167), and the old story of Heather Adams falling in Harefield's lake is retold once more (169), as is the story of the Pomfret courtship (175) and the Hopkins courtship (185), as well as mention of Dr. Ford's (205) and Tubby Fewling's (206) disappointments in love. Jessica Dean's and Aubrey Clover's kind attentions to the young Lord Mellings are also remembered by the Pomfrets, who recount the story to the Beltons and their guests (223). Gradka Bonescu turns up at the Fairweathers' dinner party, with consequent reminiscing about her early life in Barsetshire (236-45). Julian Rivers is remembered, with a story told about Mr. Belton throwing him off the property for having the temerity to try to paint Harefield House (179-80), but Alice Wicklow was welcomed and her work extolled (180).

As for material culture, it is, after all, 1958, so Margot brings her mother a gift of "several most enchanting kitchen objects in plastic of various colours . . . a pale blue plastic plate rack and a pale pink refuse container . . . made of something called (we think) polythene" and an Orlon tie that musn't be ironed as it will come to pieces (79). Further, the Beltons have an electric garage door opener (157), as well as an electric roll-up fireplace screen (173), both of which are approvingly described. Clearly, Thirkell is more accepting of change than she has been in the past and can even see some positives in it.

In personal description, there is a half-page discussion of the unattractiveness of adult feet (27), and Margot and Kate Carter have an extended exchange about the importance of good looks and the pleasure they give others (111). Rose Fairweather is, of course, as beautiful as ever (235), and Margot has become much better groomed, with some lovely designer dresses, one described lovingly as "soft grey silk pleated from neck to hem with hanging pleated sleeves and a wide belt of soft silver leather" (235), a perfect dress for a woman "who isn't young and isn't slim" (234).

Music is mentioned quite a bit in this book: Tubby Fewling sings after "the party recalled the nostalgic songs of their childhood" (29) and again by himself, feeling grateful to Handel (34). He sings again for the dinner party at the Leslies' home, where he brings some of the listeners to tears singing Handel in

Italian (52). There is a similar poignant passage of a remembrance of Mr. Macfadyen's singing Shubert several years earlier (114). Tubby later plays the piano at the Fairweathers' tea (134) and at his own dinner party (152), and he is such a music lover that when he is down-hearted, he plays the piano a lot for comfort (233).

Another charming vignette is of travel, with young people having wonderful summer vacations on the continent despite shabby cars and discomfort (62). This description is followed by a very funny one of the Misses Hampton and Bent lecturing passengers on their cruise about Lesbos, after which a college student sings "My Lesbia hath a beaming eye," which was later sung in "several quite original versions" while "nearly all the passengers said it was such a charming song and so English" (62). In this passage, Thirkell shows that she has not completely lost her touch for subtlety, wit, and malice, as the Bishop is made fun of and the oblivious passengers innocently admire a song made salacious by mischievous young people, encouraged by Hampton and Bent. Altogether, that is a lot of meaning to be transferred in a few very innocuous sentences that seem to say something entirely different.

Love At All Ages (1959)

Love at All Ages is an unsettled book right from its beginning. It opens again, very comfortingly, at a party at Mrs. Morland's house in High Rising, but is built on the very thin premise of a possible pony club in that village, although none of the protagonists is very interested in either ponies or riding. By page 12, "everyone lost interest," although the idea keeps coming up, to no avail. Mrs. Morland forgets to even mention it on her visit to The Towers (56), although The Duchess of Towers later tells Giles Foster and his mother that Mrs. Morland, who doesn't ride and has no young children, wants to start the pony club (73). Oddly enough, Roddy Wicklow, despite his statement that High Rising is "all elderly married people whose children are out in the world," decides to go over unasked and help Giles try to organize the pony club there, since Roddy is "fairly free" (86), but the interest is not there and it all comes to nothing (93). Thirkell is still laying it on with a trowel about the unselfishness, exhaustion, and hard work of the Pomfrets (63), perhaps because their agent "has nothing particular to do" (86).

Very early it is apparent that the Duke of Towers, his family, and his Towers, briefly mentioned in *A Double Affair* and *Close*

Quarters, will be protagonists. For readers coming to the books after Thirkell's death and knowing there will be no more after the next one, *Three Score and Ten*, there is something very irritating about having to learn a whole new cast of characters this late in the series; it was one thing to meet the Hallidays and the Grantlys after the war, then to meet another new family, the Crosses, in 1955, but at least they each appeared in several books. In addition, there is the annoyance of The Towers being so close in name with Pomfret Towers, a much more confusing situation than Bateman being Colonel Crofts' batman, which is endlessly noted throughout many books as being somehow confusing.

The Towers is noted as being of the same period as Pomfret Towers, with even more awful details: "[F]or sheer glory of unadulterated hideosity . . . it had no rival (18-19, 48, 57). The description of the house where the Duke and Duchess of Towers live, having rented out The Towers, is much more appealing, as the brick, the proportions, the elegant carved fireplaces and the beautiful windows are cited, as are the carpets and the furniture (49). Additionally, the long drawing room is exceptionally beautiful with its white carved paneling and bay window, French door to the garden, and painting by Millais (52). The beauty of Nutfield, with its lovely stone bridge, elegant curved road, and Georgian houses, is again detailed, (106).

The English countryside is described idyllically and compared to a "Constable landscape," after which the Duke says he has a Constable painting that he shall probably have to sell, much to Sir Edmund Pridham's dismay, and the Duke holds out hope of a rich American buyer (39-40, 56). Further views are of the Golden Valley, "perhaps one of the most romantic views in Barsetshire . . . at the early evening hour . . .all very [George] Morland (283). The peace and loveliness of the Close (218-219) are emphasized, but all is not so lovely: there is a description of a rare and hideous plant, Fibrositiss Vomitaria, which sounds suspiciously like Palafox Borealis from the Old Bank House (131).

Americans are center stage in *Love at All Ages*, and they are no more believable than ever and considerably more folksy (66, 143, 145, 223). Lee Sumter, of South Carolina, invites Lady Elaine to visit his mother in America shortly after meeting her (252-53). Franklin, the American Duchess of Towers, is rather overdone, portrayed as bossy, open-handed, and kind, with an extremely casual way of speaking. She knows the songs of the Civil War and can play "Frankie and Johnny" on the guitar (50-51). Thirkell has gotten criticism over the years for writing that the Duchess of Towers, an American from Lumberville, Virginia, has "New England good breeding" (234), but there is no reason why she couldn't have a father from there, as her mother is from Franklinsville, Georgia. More problematic is the stereotyping of Americans, to the extent that Thirkell mocks herself, having Robert Leslie, who is enchanted by the Duchess, having "a strong suspicion that the Duchess was putting over an American act for his benefit" (116) and later having the Dowager Duchess of Towers "gently parodying" Lee Sumter (248). Another American, the wealthy Woolcott van Dryven, buys hideous art from the Duke, leaving one to wonder about the former's taste and the latter's good luck (21).

There is a lot of repetitive nostalgia, including Lord Mellings' attention from Aubrey Clover and Jessica Dean (57, 60-61, 170, 273), and concern for him is expressed many, many times (188). He is doing well at Sandhurst, but, in keeping with much of the British upper class, even now, there is no university for him (69), nor for Giles, who, much like the late Princess Diana later, does not even finish school (*Three Score and Ten*). Lavinia Merton's further education will consist of a long visit to a French family, where she will, like Margaret Tebben over twenty years earlier, presumably pick up some polish and cooking skills (*Love at All Ages* 70), and Emily Foster will have a year at a finishing school in Paris (110). Clearly the upper classes have no need of credentialism.

The Thatchers of Grumpers End at Pomfret Madrigal are remembered in detail (59), and so is Mrs. Brandon's remark about needing a Bishop the community can dislike (81). The well worn story of the bell and the fish in the Bishop's garden is again related (118), as is the story of Noel Merton's infatuation with Mrs. Arbuthnot, twice (160, 165). Lord Stoke giving the pearl necklace to Edith Graham is remembered (191, 205), and Mrs. Rivers and her work are recalled with contempt (188). Noel Merton relates the tale of Lady Cora Palliser rushing Sir Cecil Waring to the hospital (271), and the group dining at the White Hart after the Oriel wedding have a fine time nostalgically recalling the Follies songs of the past (257). The weekend house party of *Pomfret Towers* is remembered again and again (285, 292, 300, 309), and Lydia Merton regales a group with the transformation of Margot Phelps (297). Oddly enough, Lord Pomfret, who has previously had tender feelings for Lydia, says here that she "is a remarkable woman for whom I have considerable respect even if she does rather lord it over one," while Lady Pomfret, who has hitherto shown no interest in Noel says that he "always gives me a delightful feeling that he may ask me to elope with him" (308). Finally, Lydia gives Noel a full replay of the Dunkirk telegram that came in the closing pages of *Cheerfulness Breaks In* (*Love at All Ages* 310).

Re the fine arts, a nice little conversation takes place between Mr. Oriel and Mrs. Crawley about art and how it dates, as she notes that Arundel prints look old-fashioned, just as Medici reproductions did for an earlier generation (158-59). Everard Carter expresses his displeasure with cubist painting (157). The Dowager Duchess of Towers paints watercolors and is aware enough to imply that people only buy them because she has a title (222). Further on, the Fieldings discuss themed Victorian painting (226), and throughout, music brings Ludo and Lavinia together several times (76-77, 300, 304), laying the foundation for deep affection.

As she did in *Close Quarters*, Thirkell seems to admire modern comfort. She applauds the small, new kitchen at Pomfret Towers, and gives a peroration on the three things needed for "real comfort": good heating, good food, and good beds (193). Similarly, there is lengthy description of the comforts and good food of the White Hart (251).

Thirkell exhibits the assumption of being fluent in French and German, as well as having Lord Mellings opine on French and German literature (269, 276). A nice wit appears in Thirkell's characters' admiration of Rudyard Kipling's poetry, since he is a cousin of hers (272), and in her own reference to the works of J. M. Barrie, her godfather (281).

Personal descriptions are as present as ever. Harry and Jessica Merton seem to be clones of Giles and Emily Foster (270). Edith Graham appears again, now Lord William Harcourt's wife, and in a less prominent role. Here she seems to be simply a vessel for Thirkell to give her usual delightful descriptions of babies (30, 32, 56, 115-16, 126-27). In a moment reminiscent of David Leslie, Lydia Merton recognizes in her husband Noel "a slight boredom—a malady which was apt to overtake him occasionally, for he did not suffer fools with any enthusiasm" (202). Similarly, Lady Fielding feels that "her husband's patience might give way at any moment" and quickly bids the company goodbye (229).

There is some uncertainty about Lavinia Merton's age, as she is "fifteen or so" at one point (61), then seventeen a few pages later (69), then "not yet seventeen" even later (162). At one point the Pomfrets, watching Lavinia Merton and her family leave, say it is a good thing for Ludo to have a "female friend of his own age" (212), but that is not actually Lavinia, since she announces later that she is sixteen (265). There are other inconsistencies, such as the location of the Oriels' honeymoon, first Cap Ferrat, courtesy of the Pomfrets (141), then later changed to "several cathedral cities" (225), and lastly said to be Brighton (246). Although in A Double Affair the Pomfrets have hired Miss Updike to replace Miss Merriman as their secretary, Miss Updike seems to have turned into Miss Cowshay (277). The Dowager Duchess of Towers hardly knows the de Courcys (254), but a few pages later says that Lady de Courcy is an old friend with whom she is going to stay (259). Lord Mellings is out when Lavinia Merton calls him, but is in a few lines later and talks to her (262). Lady Graham is apparently driving herself, whereas in earlier books she has to be driven (119), and she gives a long dissertation about her nephew Martin Leslie's missing foot (125-26), when Martin simply has a limp from the war and Thirkell is clearly thinking of Robin Dale's foot. But as Emerson so truly says, "Consistency is the hobgoblin of little minds." More consistency is provided by the weather, which is mostly pretty dreadful, and Thirkell writes often about it (106, 166-168, 175, 180, 208, 213, 294).

There is a charming vintage Thirkell sidebar describing the vagaries of fashion (216), as there is also one about the joys of grandmotherhood (219). In her Laura Morland alter ego, Thirkell has more to say about authorship, and by this time the remarks seem to have some truth in them:

> "I HATE having to write [my books] and I would sooner DIE, but I can't afford not to, so every year I very ANGRILY write another one." (152)

Given Thirkell's comments reported in Strickland (171) about the process of writing *Love at All Ages*, one can well believe these sentiments are not just Mrs. Morland's.

Three Score and Ten (1961)

Three Score and Ten is generally accepted to have the first five chapters written by Thirkell, with the rest of the book by C. A. LeJeune, so the portion beyond page 133 will be assumed to be LeJeune, who does a fine job in finishing the Barsetshire chronicles very much in Thirkell fashion. Despite some critics' feeling otherwise, the biggest difference between their sections seems to have been LeJeune's introduction in Chapter 6 of a Morland grandson, Robin, who is the vehicle for the very hilarious description of stream of consciousness writing (Thirkell's "divagations") (202-03). Clearly, LeJeune is both amusing herself and paying tribute to Thirkell's own sense of humor. Robin, son and clone of Tony Morland, is a main character of the rest of the book, but Mrs. Morland is, of course, the centerpiece for both writers. There has been speculation that Thirkell intended Sylvia Gould to marry Lord Stoke, but, closing the circle, LeJeune brings her together in this last book, finally, with Dr. Ford, to whom she was engaged in *Demon in the House*, near the beginning of the Barsetshire saga.

Three Score and Ten opens with tea, yet again, at Mrs. Morland's house in High Rising with the usual cast of the Knoxes, the Coateses, Lord Stoke, and Stoker the cook. Another comforting echo of the past is the description of Winter Overcotes station and its two female porters with their tight clothes, ever-present cigarettes, and helpful kindness (114-15). Additionally Winston Churchill's visit to the Great Conservative Rally is mentioned fondly (131-32).

The nostalgia goes on and on: Lord Stoke remembers Tony Morland's long-ago visit to Rising Castle (11, 44, 88), the author recalls Tony's friendship with the Vicarage girls Rose and Dora Gould (69-73), Anne Knox remembers Mrs. Rivers' books (7, 105), and Mrs. Morland and Lord Stoke remember his love for Edith Thorne (18, 31, 40, 83). There is a mild reference to a possible previous proposal by Lord Stoke to Mrs. Morland (31), although Mrs. Morland denies it (53), [in addition to her previous offers from Adrian Coates, George Knox, and Lord Crosse].

Mrs. Morland gives Sylvia Gould a speech about growing up in a house without a bathroom, where servants carried up bath water, concluding nostalgically that "The big houses had lots of servants—which is really the answer to everything" (85). The life of the past with no proper bathroom is lauded later, in a long, nostalgic passage descriptive of

Thirkell's youth (125), and a very touching reference is made to the death of her own young daughter (130).

Lord and Lady Bond, along with the Dowager Duchess of Towers, alternate visiting Lord Stoke, providing an opportunity for reminiscence about events from *Before Lunch* (95, 47-48). Other reminiscences relate to Jessica Dean and Aubrey Clover, and the playlet they put on for the Northbridge coronation fete (119), and to the circumstances of Miss Sowerby's handing over of the Old Bank House to Mr. Sam Adams many years earlier (126-27). The marriage of Canon Fewling and Margot Phelps is given attention, as is that of Edith Graham to Lord William Harcourt (130).

Aesthetics seem much less important than usual in this book, and so most description is less vivid than in previous books. Two more negative perorations are given, both bearing on the unattractiveness of adult bare feet (10, 113). More positively, there is appreciation of old oriental rugs (29), and nostalgia for the system of old-fashioned bell pulls (38), old-fashioned candy (43), early movies (43), and Mrs. Morland's early schooling (110-11). Mrs. Morland recalls the paintings at Staple Park, home of the Bonds, as "mostly bad but highly varnished copies of second-rate Old Masters" (49).

There is some confusion about Staple Park, the home of the Bonds: Lady Bond, the former Daphne Stonor, talks of her son inheriting the property, then says she wishes her brother Denis had married and had a son "to carry on" (103), but, in fact, the property descends through her husband's side of the family, so any child of Denis Stonor would be completely irrelevant. Staple Park itself is described by its mistress as not "so awful" as it used to be (100), but there is not much description of Rising Castle.

Descriptive divagations on limping, umbrellas, attics, books, dress stands, and hospitals abound (55-59), with a long and tedious description of bagging sweets and pushing the service trolley around the little cottage hospital (60-68). One oddity at this stage of the book is that Mrs. Morland has three sons at one point (63), but then reverts a few pages later to her usual four sons (68).

In regards to literature, there is a long reference to Robert Browning's "Soliloquy of the Spanish Cloister" with attendant divagations (79), and references to other writers, including Dickens, Thackeray, and Scott (99). In one discussion of literature, Lord Stoke complains in a hilariously philistine manner of Swinburne's writing, "I don't know why he did it—[he] came of a good family . . ." (12-13).

In keeping with Thirkell's interest in comfort and her late-blooming tolerance of modernity in aid of same, she admires the idea of a small, snug house that is easy to heat and has a modern kitchen and bathroom, an attached garage, and a new water heater (22). As in *Close Quarters*, Thirkell in her old age is more interested in comfort, efficiency, and convenience than she has been in the past. She continues that interest in comfort with an enthusiastic description of the delicious home grown food at Lord Stoke's lunch (94).

As often in previous books, Mrs. Morland mouths the author's opinions about the writing life, especially in the passage bemoaning how difficult it is to keep all the characters and their ages straight, and appreciating how much the typist helps catch errors (80). Mrs. Morland says she expects to "go on writing another nice book like the last one till I die," a poignant remark under the circumstances, and a further discussion of authors includes not only Mrs. Morland but Mrs. Rivers as well (104-05).

CHAPTER VI: CONCLUSION

Thirkell's creation of the world of Barsetshire stands as a tribute to her abilities and taste. She is a fine writer who evokes a cherished English past that is very dear to many readers of various nationalities and ethnicities. Her idealized portraits of life in the bucolic English countryside have tapped into traditional archetypes, written though the books were during some of England's most difficult years, those of the Depression, World War II, and the unsettled postwar years.

It is, perhaps, too harsh to condemn out of hand her constant repetitions in the later books of events of the previous books. Aside from being an excellent writer, Thirkell was savvy enough to know that not every reader would read the books in chronological order (departure from this preferred method became especially the case as many of the books went out of print at various times). Additionally, Susan Scanlon points out that "At some points [Angela Thirkell] is referencing events that happened 20+ years earlier. This may have served to remind readers who all these people were. For us [members of the Angela Thirkell Society] it's simpler, as many of us have read all the books over just months or a few years instead of over 26 years" (private letter).

In closing, one finds after examining all twenty-nine Barsetshire books, that there are very clear changes in Thirkell's attitude toward aesthetics and toward nostalgia in the pre-war, wartime, and post-war books. In a long passage from *Love Among the Ruins*, comparing the rise of the large, talented and wealthy Dean family to the decline of the highly strung Fosters/Pomfrets, Thirkell is clearly mellowing in her views, and is hopeful about the future, recognizing and accepting change (123-24). Laura Collins rightly emphasizes that although Thirkell's characters increasingly look back, "they cope; and most of them change and adjust to the Horrible Brave New World" (129).

English poet U. A. Fanthorpe, talking about herself in an interview, might well have been talking about Thirkell when Fanthorpe said of herself:

> I'm so old that I remember the last war when I was a child growing up and therefore I remember England as under siege, a feeling of bombs being about to drop and things of that sort. And that meant, for some reason, the impact on me was the specialness of England and the English language.

Although Thirkell is known for being politically conservative in her books, it would be interesting to know just how much of her complaining and resisting change is a function of the war and the years of Labour government, and how much is simply a function of aging, and preference for the familiar, as happens to all of us. The concern for aesthetics generally grows with the passage of time [with the exception of the final book], as in Thirkell's view a thing of beauty clearly is a joy forever. As for nostalgia, with the earlier books, there is a strong sense of personal loss for loved ones, but by the postwar books, that sense of loss and nostalgia is for an entire civilization which has changed enormously.

Works Cited

Armstrong, Nancy. *Desire and Domestic Fiction: A Political History of the Novel*. Oxford & New York: Oxford University Press, 1987.

Burrell, Barbara. *Angela Thirkell's World: A Complete Guide to the People and Places of Barsetshire*. Wickford, RI: Moyer Bell, 2001.

Chapman, H. W. Review of *Private Enterprise*, by Angela Thirkell. *The Spectator*. 5 Dec. 1947. 179:722.

Collins, Laura Roberts. *English Country Life in the Barsetshire Novels of Angela Thirkell*. Westport, CT: Greenwood, 1994.

Fanthorpe, Ursula Askham. Interview in *Poetry Archive* qtd. by Robert Barr. Retrieved May 2, 2009 from apnews.excite.com/article/20090501/D97TH9TG2.html

Fritzer. Penelope. *Ethnicity and Gender in the Barsetshire Novels of Angela Thirkell*. Westport, CT: Greenwood, 1999.

Gill, Richard. *Happy Rural Seat: The English Country House and the Literary Imagination*. New Haven and London: Yale University Press, 1972.

Hornby, Nick. *Shakespeare Wrote for Money*. San Francisco: Believer Books, 2008.

Jutland Cottage, review of, by Angela Thirkell. *The New Yorker*. 24 Oct. 1953. 29:159.

Kynaston, David. *Austerity Britain, 1945-1951*. London: Bloomsbury Publishing PLC, 2008.

Langstaff, Eleanor. "Angela Margaret Thirkell," in *An Encyclopedia of British Women Writers.* ed by Paul Schlueter and Jane Schlueter. Hamden, CT: Garland Publishing, 1988: 445-46.

Levin, Jill. *The "Land of Lost Content":Sex, Art, and Class in the Novels of Angela Thirkell, 1933-1960*. Thesis. Washington University, 1986.

Mather, Rachel R. *The Heirs of Jane Austen: Twentieth Century Writers and the Comedy of Manners.* New York: Peter Lang, 1996.

Moor, Christopher. Personal interview. February 11, 2009.

Nesbitt, Jennifer Poulos. *Narrative Settlements: Geographies of British Women's Fiction Between the Wars*. Toronto: University of Toronto Press, 2005.

Scanlon, Susan. Private letter. May, 31, 2009.

Snowden, Cynthia. *Going to Barsetshire: A Companion to the Barsetshire Novels of Angela Thirkell*. Kearny, NE: Morris Publishing, 2000.

Strickland, Margot. *Angela Thirkell, Portrait of a Lady Novelist*. London: Gerald Duckworth & Co., 1977. 2nd printing Angela Thirkell Society North America. Kearny, NE: Morris Publishing, 1996.

Thirkell, Angela. *August Folly*. Long Preston, England: Magna Large Print Books, 1993 [orig. 1936].

Thirkell, Angela. *Before Lunch*. London: Hamish Hamilton, 1949 [orig. 1939].

Thirkell, Angela. *The Brandons*. New York: Alfred P. Knopf, 1939.

Thirkell, Angela. *Cheerfulness Breaks In*. New York: Carroll & Graf, 1990 [orig. 1940].

Thirkell, Angela. *Close Quarters*. New York: Alfred Knopf, 1958.

Thirkell, Angela. *County Chronicle*. London: Hamish Hamilton, 1950.

Thirkell, Angela. *The Demon in the House*. Wakefield, R. I: Moyer Bell, 1996 [orig. 1934].

Thirkell, Angela. *A Double Affair*. London: Hamish Hamilton, 1957.

Thirkell, Angela. *The Duke's Daughter*. London: Hamish Hamilton, 1951.

Thirkell, Angela. *Enter Sir Robert*. New York: Alfred A. Knopf, 1955.

Thirkell, Angela. *Growing Up*. New York: Alfred A. Knopf, 1944 [orig. 1943].

Thirkell, Angela. *Happy Return*. New York: Alfred A. Knopf, 1952.

Thirkell, Angela. *The Headmistress*. New York: Alfred A. Knopf, 1945 [orig.1944].

Thirkell, Angela. *High Rising*. New York: Carroll & Graf, 1989 [orig. 1933].

Thirkell, Angela. *Jutland Cottage*. London: Hamish Hamilton, 1953.

Thirkell, Angela. *Love Among the Ruins*. Wakefield, R. I.: Moyer-Bell, 1997 [orig. 1947].

Thirkell, Angela. *Love at All Ages*. New York: Alfred Knopf, 1959.

Thirkell, Angela. *Marling Hall*. London: Hamish Hamilton, 1942.

Thirkell, Angela. *Miss Bunting*. New York: Alfred A. Knopf, 1946 [orig. 1945].

Thirkell, Angela. *Never Too Late*. New York: Alfred A. Knopf, 1956.

Thirkell. Angela. *Northbridge Rectory*. New York: Carroll & Graf, Publishers, 1969 [orig. 1941].

Thirkell, Angela. *The Old Bank House*. London: Hamish Hamilton, 1949.

Thirkell, Angela. *Peace Breaks Out*. London: Hamish Hamilton, 1946.

Thirkell, Angela. *Pomfret Towers*. London: Hamish Hamilton, 1938.

Thirkell, Angela. *Private Enterprise*. New York: Alfred A. Knopf, 1948 [orig. 1947].

Thirkell, Angela. *Summer Half*. London: Hamish Hamilton, 1949 [orig. 1937].

Thirkell, Angela and C. A. LeJeune. *Three Score and Ten*. New York: Alfred A. Knopf, 1962. [orig. 1961].

Thirkell, Angela. *What Did It Mean?* London: Hamish Hamilton, 1954.

Thirkell, Angela. *Wild Strawberries*. London: Hamish Hamilton, 1952 [orig. 1932].

Walbridge, E. F. Review of *Close Quarters*, by Angela Thirkell. *Library Journal*. 1 Sept. 1958. 83:2323.

Index

Acacia House, 121
Adams, Heather
  (Pilward), 53, 75,
  81, 82, 123
Adams, Sam, 6, 9, 49,
  50, 53, 68, 69, 76,
  87, 97, 136
Americans, 128
Anglican service, 5,
  12, 53
Architecture, 85, 102
Arcot House, 48, 122
Armstrong, Nancy, 9
Babies, 111
Banks, Miss, 60
Barchester Cathedral,
  5, 73, 121
Barrie, J. M., 131
Barton, Alice, 21, 22,
  123
Barton, Guy, 33
Beliers Priory, 5, 8,
  25, 44, 45, 78, 79,
  84, 90
Belton, Charles, 16,
  19, 49, 67, 78, 86
Belton, Elsa (Hornby),
  48, 78, 87
Bent, Miss, 74, 88,
  109, 125
Bingham, Rose
  (Leslie), 61

Birkett, Geraldine
  (Fairweather), 11,
  47, 106
Birkett, Rose
  (Fairweather), 11,
  14, 19, 47, 61, 75,
  85, 87, 88, 91, 92,
  96, 106, 109, 116,
  123, 124, 135
Birkett, William Henry,
  19, 47, 63, 64, 96
Bishop of Barchester,
  9, 15, 39, 73, 74,
  84, 94, 103, 116,
  125, 130
Bond, Lord Alured, 27,
  28, 136, 137
Bonescu, Gradka, 66,
  123
Bowen, Elizabeth, 7
Brandon Abbey, 24,
  26, 45
Brandon, Amelia, 24
Brandon, Francis, 24,
  65, 109
Brandon, Lavinia
  (Joram), 24, 129,
  131, 132
Browning, Robert, 137
Bunting, Maude, 30,
  51, 54, 60, 66
Burrell, Barbara, 119
Canaletto (Giovanni
  Antonio Canal), 86

Carter, Everard, 65, 110, 131

Carter, Mrs. Richard, 110

Cary, Joyce, 7

Cedars, The, 80

Chapman, H. W., 101

Children, 68

Christie, Agatha, 7

Clover, Aubrey, 93, 95, 96, 123, 129, 136

Coates, Adrian, 12, 35, 135

Collier, John, 23

Collins, Laura Roberts, 1, 140

Constable, John, 128

Crawley, Grace, 79, 82, 85, 86, 112

Crawley, Jane, 51, 52, 53, 54, 112

Crawley, Octavia (Needham), 46

Crockett, Selena (Hopkins), 46, 95

Crofts, 9, 91, 127

Crosse, John-Arthur, 99, 106, 113

Crosse, Lord (John), 104, 107, 135

Dale, Dr., 53, 54

Dale, Isabel (Silverbridge), 56, 70, 71, 73, 74, 77, 79, 81, 113

Dale, Robin, 74, 133

Dean, Helen (Fanshawe), 18

Dean, Jessica, 72, 93, 95, 123, 129, 132, 136

Dean, Lawrence, 18, 91

Dean, Susan (Belton), 65, 80, 114, 139, 143

Dickens, Charles, 16, 137

Dowlah Cottage, 47, 79

Eileen (Bateman), 108

Fairweather, Geoff, 47

Fanshawe, Charles, 19

Fanthorpe, Ursula Askem, 140

Feeder, Mrs., 91, 110

Fewling, George (Tubby), 89, 91, 117, 119, 120, 121, 123, 124, 136

Fielding, Anne, 11, 51, 55, 57, 59, 60, 74, 87, 135

Ford, Dr., 14, 123, 134

Foster, Giles (Lord Pomfret), 20, 21, 27, 94, 95, 130

Foster, Giles (son of Lord Pomfret), 17, 70, 126, 129, 132

149

Fritzer, Penelope, 85, 99, 120
Garcia, Senor, 111
Gatherum Castle, 5, 8, 25, 70, 73, 79
Gill, Richard, 6, 7
Gould, Dora, 14, 135
Graham, Clarissa (Belton), 60, 66, 67, 78, 81, 85, 86, 96, 104, 115
Graham, Edith (Harcourt), 99, 103, 104, 108, 113, 119, 130, 132, 136
Graham, Lady (Agnes Leslie), 16, 66, 110
Grant, Hilary, 27
Grantly, Eleanor (Keith), 95
Grantly, Grace (Lufton), 79, 82, 85, 86, 112
Grantly, Tom, 15, 56, 75, 76, 78, 81, 99
Great House at Allington, 74
Green, Henry, 7
Gresham, Jane, 51, 53, 54, 115
Grey, Una, 12, 15
Hallbury, 51
Halliday, Eleanor, 95
Halliday, George, 99, 102, 103, 106, 112, 118

Halliday, Sylvia (Leslie), 1, 56, 57, 60, 81, 111, 116, 117, 134, 135
Hampton, Miss, 88, 109, 125
Harcourt, Lady Elaine, 128
Harcourt, Lord William, 119, 132, 136
Harefield, 47, 67, 78, 86, 91, 122, 123
Harefield Park, 47
Harvey, Geoffrey, 5, 15, 40, 42, 62, 77
Hatch End, 58, 100, 102, 107, 108, 117
Hatch House, 58
Heath, Nurse, 111
Hibberd, Sir Ogilvy, 15, 27, 58, 111
Hoare, Mrs., 50
Holden, Mr., 35, 43, 92, 93
Holdings, 103, 110
Holt, C. W., 103, 109
Holtby, Winifred, 1
Hornby, Christopher, 6, 48, 78, 87
Hornby, Nick, 8
Hovis House, 116
Hubback, 111
Huxley, Aldous, 6
Isherwood, Christopher, 6

James, Henry, 7
Joram, Dr. William
    (Colonial Bishop,
    Canon), 70, 73, 75,
    86
Keith, Colin, 20, 33,
    43, 62, 94, 98
Keith, Kate (Carter),
    20, 92, 110, 124
Kipling, Rudyard, 41,
    131
Knox, George, 11, 12,
    13, 18, 135
Knox, Sybil, 11, 38
Kynaston, David, 54
Labour government,
    54, 55, 64, 69, 83,
    89, 141
Langstaff, Eleanor, 2
Lawrence, D. H., 6
Lazarus College, 24
Leslie, David, 5, 42,
    55, 57, 60, 62, 92,
    115, 117, 118, 132
Leslie, Emmy
    (Grantly), 59, 66,
    67, 77, 81, 82, 104
Leslie, Gay, 17
Leslie, Giles, 17
Leslie, Henry, 7, 50
Leslie, John, 17, 23,
    32, 71, 90, 99, 106,
    113
Leslie, Lady Emily, 17,
    85, 102, 103, 111,
    115

Leslie, Martin, 17, 66,
    76, 117, 133
Leslie, Robert, 14, 99,
    100, 102, 107, 109,
    115, 129, 137
Levin, Jill, 22, 113
Lodge, The, 78, 80
Lufton, Justinia, 92
Lufton, Lord
    (Ludovic), 79, 81,
    85, 118
Lufton, Maria
    (Marling), 81
Lytton, Neville, 23
Macfadyen, Donald,
    92, 118, 119, 122,
    125
Macpherson, Mr., 5,
    59, 79, 81
Margett, Jasper, 46
Marigold, 81, 84
Marling, Lucy
    (Adams), 6, 53, 66,
    67, 72, 75, 76, 81,
    97
Marling, Oliver, 6, 39,
    71, 73, 76, 80, 81,
    85
Marling, Willliam, 40
Mather, Rachel, 90
Mellings, Lord
    (Ludovic Foster),
    106, 123, 129, 131,
    133
Merivale, Mrs., 52
Millers, The, 9, 85

Moor, Christopher, 60
Morland, Laura, 133
Morland, Tony, 11,
    12, 13, 14, 15, 19,
    109, 134, 135
Music, 124
Needham, Tommy,
    43, 46
Nesbitt, Jennifer
    Poulos, 1, 30, 90
Northbridge, 30, 32,
    33, 34, 37, 38, 39,
    43, 92, 93, 94, 98,
    108, 116, 121, 136
Norton, Lady, 9, 15
Nutfield, 20, 127
Old Bank House, 5, 6,
    62, 68, 69, 75, 86,
    97, 128, 136
Old Manor House,
    102, 107
Omnium, Duke of
    (Plantagenet
    Palliser), 79, 122
Orwell, George, 16
Palliser, Lady Cora
    (Waring), 45, 56,
    70, 75, 77, 78, 79,
    80, 81, 85, 91, 93,
    96, 117, 130
Parkinsons, 9, 122
Paxon, Minnie, 94
Pemberton, Ianthe,
    26, 35, 38, 94, 97,
    98

Peters (butler), 103,
    109
Pettinger, Bertha, 50
Phelps, Admiral, 111,
    120
Phelps, Margot
    (Macfadyen,
    Fewling), 88, 89,
    91, 110, 118, 119,
    120, 122, 123, 124,
    130, 136
Phelps, Mrs., 111
Plassey House, 47, 80
Pollett, Ed, 28, 41
Pomfret Towers, 5, 8,
    11, 20, 23, 25, 33,
    45, 73, 90, 94, 96,
    98, 103, 105, 109,
    116, 117, 122, 127,
    130, 131
Pomfret, Lady (Edith
    Thorne), 135
Pomfret, Lady (Sally
    Wicklow Foster), 22,
    114, 116, 130
Pomfret, Lord (7th
    Earl), 20, 21, 27,
    94, 95, 130
Pomfret, Lord (8th Earl
    Giles Foster), 126
Preston, Mary (Leslie),
    17, 92
Pridham, Sir Edmund,
    41, 65, 112, 128
Proctor, Thea, 23

Punshions, 97, 98, 108

Raeburn, Sir Henry, 50, 91

Richmond, George, 86, 92, 117

Rivers, Julian, 22, 23, 24, 109, 123

Rivers, Phoebe, 33

Rushwater, 16, 59, 66, 67, 76, 77, 80, 81, 117

Sackville-West, Vita, 1, 6

Sargent, John Singer, 23

Scanlon, Susan, 114, 115, 139

Scatcherd, Mr. (artist), 58, 59, 92, 101, 111, 116

Scott, Sir Walter, 137

Set of Five, 23, 24

Seymour, Miranda, 8

Shaw, George Bernard, 6

Silverbridge (town), 56, 71, 79, 80

Silverbridge, Lord (Jeffrey Palliser), 56, 71, 79

Snowden, Cynthia, 11, 99

Southbridge School, 5, 15, 32, 45, 60, 74, 82, 87, 90, 106, 108, 121

Sowerby, Miss, 69, 136

Sparling, Madeleine, 48, 50

Staple Park, 27, 136, 137

Stoke, Lord, 112, 130, 134, 135, 136, 137, 138

Stonor, Daphne (Lady Bond), 137

Stonor, Denis, 28, 137

Strickland, Margot, 4, 110, 118

Sumter, Lee, 128

Swan, Eric, 78, 82, 84, 85, 86, 92

Swinburne, Algernon Charles, 137

Tebben, Margaret (Dean), 18, 118, 119, 129

Tebben, Mr., 76

Tebben, Richard, 66

Tebben, Winifred, 1, 26

Thackeray, William Makepeace, 137

Thatcher, Doris, 68

Thatcher, Edna, 68

Thatcher, Sid, 82

Thirkell, Lance, 13

Todd, Anne, 11

Towers, Dowager
Duchess of
(Harcourt), 5, 8, 11,
21, 23, 25, 90, 96,
98, 105, 116, 126,
127, 128, 131, 136
Towers, Duchess of
(Frankie Harcourt),
128
Towers, Duke of
(Harcourt), 97, 126
Turner, Poppy, 9, 35,
36, 94, 95, 98
Twicker, Nanny, 64
Uranus, 60
Villars, Verena, 35,
36, 37, 38, 39, 43,
92, 93
Walbridge, E. F., 88
Waring, Lady Harriet,
107

Waring, Leslie
(Winter), 43, 47, 87
Waring, Sir Harry, 47
Warner, Sylvia
Townsend, 1
Waugh, Evelyn, 6, 7
Wesendonck, Robert,
14
West, Rebecca, 1, 7
Wickham, Mr., 71, 77,
91, 105, 120, 122
Wicklow, Sally Foster
(Lady Pomfret), 22,
27
Winter, Philip, 20, 43,
47, 66, 78, 82, 87,
92, 135
Winthrop, Mr., 80
Wodehouse, P. G., 7
Woolf, Virginia, 1, 7
Yeats, William Butler,
7